To Richard & … ry
Best to y…

Homer Hudelson

Homer's Odyssey: A Memoir

by Homer Hudelson

Published by Homer Hudelson

Table of Contents

3

Acknowledgments

I wrote this memoir to pass on my life experiences to our family, children, grandchildren, and great grandchild. I began this story describing my youth in the beautiful city of San Francisco. Working for the Southern Pacific Railroad – one day after I graduated from Sacred Heart High School in 1952 – was a wonderful experience, like traveling with my mother on the train. The next rewarding job I had was with the San Francisco Police Department until my retirement in 1988 after thirty years.

After my retirement from the police department, I was employed with United Airlines working in ground support for ten years, retiring at sixty-five years of age. With United Airlines, Gloria and I and our youngest son, Joseph (because he was under eighteen of age), enjoyed many flight experiences to various parts of the world.

First, I wish to thank my beautiful wife, Gloria, who has been with me for over sixty years in our marriage, who had to listen to my stories more than one once. My mother and father instilled education as a priority in addition to it being a Catholic one. My mother saved newspaper articles and clippings. With her example, I also began saving them, one of which is over sixty years old. Rest in Peace, Mom, and Dad.

Next, I want to acknowledge our beautiful children, grandchildren, and great grandchildren. Also, I want to thank our youngest son, Joseph, and his wife, Kristina, who, with their English expertise, made this memoir rewarding. Thanks, too, to Joseph's Serra High School and UC Berkeley classmate, Brian Solon, for taking my many phone calls and helping me navigate this process. Next, I need to acknowledge Cathy Wedell, our second oldest child, who is busy with her own teaching job, and her husband, Robert, who also spent his time working with this endeavor.

Homer Hudelson

South San Francisco, California

August 2022

Chapter 1

The Early Years

My sister Julia and I were born during The Great Depression in San Francisco California – she on June 22, 1932 and I on December 29, 1933. My father, Homer C., divorced, married my mother, Adeline Victoria Keller. She had one child, Wendel Rudolph. She found it necessary to have her son raised by her sister, Hilda Bowen, because as a single parent and working as a telephone operator during that era, it became too difficult for her to raise her son. Later, my father indicated that he did not wish to raise him. My mother and father never told my sister nor I any reason for this.

Born in Rich Hill, Missouri, my father came to San Francisco during the Great Depression (1930s) for work and found it with the SF Chronicle Newspaper as a mailer—where the newspapers would come off the conveyor belt and be bundled for distribution.

My parents were simple people. My mother went only to the 8th grade and my father had two years of high school. They did not drink unless they were offered one socially. I never heard them use profanity and they never argued, never. My mother was an especially kind person. My father only used corporal punishment once because I teased my sister.

My mother and father both played the piano. My father would play the piano and my sister and I would sing songs such as "Embraceable You," "Harbor Lights," and "Always," to name a few.

My father built me a chin-up bar in the backyard of the house. He also built a punching bag stand in the garage where the punching bag could hang from the above stationary holder. My father could, in rhythmic style, punch the bag with his left shoulder, elbow, hand, and then repeat this same maneuver with his right hand.

Since we lived close to Ocean Beach on 48th Avenue, I would sometimes walk just a few blocks to the ocean to fish. Perch was the easy catch. On one occasion I did catch a striped bass.

Tod Powell, the SF Chronicle Sports Writer, agreed to write an article about a commercial fisherman and his boat harbored in Half Moon Bay. I was lucky enough to get a free trip on the excursion. We all caught black snapper and other fish. However, the highlight of the fishing trip for me was the 24-pound lingcod that I caught; it was almost as big as me! Mr. Powell wrote an article, with a picture of this fish and me. Not bad for an eleven-year-old.

My maternal grandfather, Ludwig Von Keller, became a barber after his arrival from Heidelberg, Germany in the 1930s. He had a barber shop on Haight Street about three houses east of Masonic

Avenue on the south side of the street. I remember him cutting my hair with the older handheld type clippers. After cutting my hair, he gave me a round, yellow, hard candy the size of a quarter with a gold wrapper. Its flavor was butterscotch—sweet and tasty. He was able to purchase a home in the outer Sunset with his meager earnings. Haircuts were at that time 25 cents and a shave 15 cents.

Sometimes we would go to his house and listen to opera singers like Enrico Caruso on a Victrola Phonograph Player where we would wind up the phonograph handle before listening to the record. Desserts and other pastries were served. My mother sang in the SF Choir and, being a Soprano, could sing a High C. My grandfather's first wife, Louisa Castro, died before I was able to meet her. My mother told me that her grandfather, Castro, was one of the first Sheriffs of San Luis Obispo, a city in California's Central Coast.

In April in 1850, Sheriff Henry J. Dalley was elected as the first Sheriff of San Luis Obispo County. Francisco Castro shortly thereafter became sheriff of San Luis Obispo.

In Fresno, California, after his arrival from Germany, my grandfather Ludwig, was trying to form a Barber's Union there when he received the notorious "Black Hand" in the mail often associated with extortion or other intimidation. Later, in his seventies and with health issues, he moved to San Jose, California and purchased a home on North First Street. His daughter Hilda and her husband lived there with him. I remember staying there one summer when I was about 13 or 14 years old to pick apricots. Pay was 10 cents for a large bucket. Three immigrants, husband, wife, and a teenage daughter, worked and lived on the orchard where they built a shack out of wooden trays (used to dry apricots) as their lodgings.

I remember coming home on the bus at around 10 o'clock from an evening show in downtown San Jose — my Aunt Hilda told me that the front door to the house would be opened but the screen door locked; the back door would be open but the back screen door unlocked. After the bus left me off I walked about four blocks to the house. There were no concerns about safety. During the summer the weather was always hot.

Sometime later, my Grandfather Ludwig passed away. At the funeral, union representatives came and showed their appreciation and respect. I inherited his automobile, a brown four-door 1934 Dodge; it had bench-type seats that I believe were more comfortable than the bucket seats in today's automobiles. It was somewhat damaged. The door handles to this vehicle were toward the front of the door, unlike the door handles of the cars of today.

I used this car to pick up two Catholic Sisters of Mercy—like the ones that taught us at Holy Name Grammar School—and drive them from their Motherhouse on Adeline Drive in Burlingame to St. Stephen's Church, located on Eucalyptus Drive in San Francisco. A neighbor friend, James Seyler, went along with me. Before driving them to their destination they said prayers for a safe journey and for my safe driving We arrived safely at St. Stephen's a short time later.

My other grandfather, William T. Hudelson, was from Kansas City Missouri, and was born in 1856. He was a medical doctor and would often take a horse and buggy to visit his patients. His obituary mentioned this and added that he often took the back roads for fear of hostile Native Americans. His wife, Mary Molly Cassidy, was from Meath, Ireland and they had seven children—six boys and one girl. I believe my grandfather had a drinking problem and they divorced. Mary died young from cancer and was forced to give up two of her children to a close friend before she passed away.

My grandfather eventually came to California and became a pharmacist. He lived with my father for a while before he died. My father and grandfather are buried side by side in Holy Cross Cemetery in Colma, California. It was said that before he died, my grandfather converted to Catholicism.

The Pacific Coast League Minor baseball games were played at Sixteenth and Bryant Street. The San Francisco Seals were the home team. I remember seeing one game when Dino Restelli, a home team player, hit a towering fly ball and when the infield gathered around the pitcher's mound to catch the ball and record the out, no one called for the ball and it dropped near the pitcher's mound with Mr. Restelli standing on third base with a triple. Hustle, O yeah.

When working odd jobs in my teenage years, I had an occasion to sweep and mop up a barbershop and next door there was a radio shop where I purchased a crystal radio with earphones. It was a simple radio receiver popular in the early days of radio that used only the power of the received radio signal to produce sound, needing no external power. I placed a copper wire antenna in the backyard and my dad and I would listen to the Seals' baseball games.

Another job I had when I was about fourteen years of age (1947) was working at a meat market on Saturdays. This was from eight in the morning until six in the evening, with an hour off for lunch. I made fifty cents an hour. One Saturday it was busy so we didn't finish work until six forty-five. I asked my boss for fifty cents for the overtime. He was visibly irritated, but gave me the fifty cents. He also told his brother, Paul Anderson, who was the chief engineer at the SF Ice Skating Rink about my request for the overtime money. Oh well!

My father, being a baseball fan, would take me to the Upper Great Highway, and in the center of the south and northbound lanes would hit fly balls to me, instructing me how to catch them.

I went to Francis Scott Key Grammar School on 43rd Avenue, and later in 1944 my sister, Julia, and I went to Holy Name Grammar School located on 40th Avenue. I entered the fourth grade and my sister the sixth grade The Catholic nuns, Sisters of Mercy, who dressed all in black, were my teachers. My father was Catholic but did not attend Mass — I believe because he was divorced. My mother was baptized a Catholic but followed the teachings of the Lutheran Church and she also did not attend church. In our first year at Holy Name we were baptized into the Catholic Faith; the tuition was $1.00 a month.

It is interesting to note that a classmate of mine at Holy Name School, Gordon Hendrickson, also became a police officer with the San Francisco Police Department. We also both became sergeants and lieutenants. We live close to each other and still see each other at the monthly Veterans' Police Officers' Association on Brotherhood Way in San Francisco.

I lived in the Outer Sunset District on 47th Avenue near Irving Street, only a few blocks from the ocean. Around and up the corner from our rented house was the Sunset Theater. My first recollection of admission to the theater in the 1930s was 5 cents. It would then increase to 7 cents, 10 cents, 12 cents, and then to 25 cents.

My parents did not own an automobile; instead, they traveled by streetcar, train, and the Greyhound Bus. In fact, I remember my cousin, Jackie, telling me that my Dad visited her and her father, Francis, his youngest brother, in Kansas City Missouri back in the 1930's, arriving there by Greyhound Bus. She further told me that she also had a sister who died in early childhood. In a letter from my cousin Mary Ellen Schmidt, it said my dad would send them weekly newspapers.

My parents later moved onto 48th Avenue, which was also in the Outer Sunset, across the street from the San Francisco Ice Arena. The rent for this house was $50.00 a month. I spent a lot of time at the ice rink because cleaning the ice after an ice skating session would entitle me to a free future admission. I helped the Chief Engineer, Paul Anderson, clean the ice after an ice-skating session to obtain my free ice-skating pass. He had been wounded in the Second World War. He was fighting on the German Front when a mortar round landed directly into the foxhole, killing his 18-year-old comrade. He told me after the explosion, he climbed out of the foxhole and ran to the first aid station. He said that he would have been killed but the enemy would rather the Americans utilize vital resources than become a casualty. Once at the first aid station, Paul was given a root beer-type glass full of whisky to numb his right arm injuries.

I met quite a few girls my age at the rink, and we became friends. While skating, lighted signs would indicate: Men only, Ladies Only, and Couples. When asking a girl to skate, we would hold hands and skate together, with music of course.

After Paul Anderson retired, a former Ice Follies Skater, Hugh Hendrickson, became one of the new owners. One day, in August 1959, Hugh went below to inspect the ice rink where a refrigerant cools the brine water, an anti-freezing agent that travels through the pipes at approximately 32 degrees so that any water placed on top of the pipes freezes and becomes the skating surface. However, this day he had a light with a chord that shorted out after some brine water splashed onto him. He was electrocuted. He was 31 years old, married, with two children. Since I had gone below to view the workings of the freezing of the ice, it made me aware of its possible dangers.

Also, to make extra money, I delivered the Shopping News twice a week on Wednesdays and Saturdays delivering over a thousand newspapers. On Saturdays, those of us delivering the newspapers would meet in the schoolyard at Francis Scott Key Grammar School located on 43rd Avenue, to receive payment. Pay was distributed in a little small brown envelope containing a two-dollar bill and 25 cents. Who would think that 50 years later when checking for Social Security contributions that the amounts would qualify for benefits?

Playland at the Beach, an amusement park located in the Outer Richmond District, was another place for entertainment. Some of the fun rides included: Chute-the-Chutes—a flat bottom boat that slid down a ramp into a body of water, The Big Dipper—a roller coaster, Bumper Cars, slides that first required you to slip into a gunny sack before using the slide, and fun games. 'The Laughing Lady"—Laughing Sal—continued laughing in her display case at the amusement park.

Great food was also a part of the amusement park biz – the famous Hot House was known for authentic Mexican food. I even washed dishes there on one occasion. Sweets like cotton candy and candy apples were sold there too. Various nickelodeons were also prevalent and for a nickel you could hear a variety of music. Lots of fun.

H.2.O: Stories Involving Water

Swimming became a significant part of my life and is still, even to this day. The Fleishhacker Pool was located near the SF Zoo at the end of Sloat Blvd., and as of 1925, was one of the largest outdoor swimming pools in the world. It contained salt water from the ocean. A diving board and a platform for diving situated at 33 feet high made this intimidating. One time my father jumped off the platform feet first. I did go up to the top of the platform to look down at the water. It was intimidating and not for me.

Sutro Baths was another swimming pool I frequented. It was located at the end of Geary Blvd near Lands' End. This pool had seven separate heated pools with swings, slides, and diving boards. To gain admission to the swimming pool and to the ice skating rink, which was also below, one had to go down ninety-nine stairs. Finally, Crystal Plunge, located on Lombard Street, provided another opportunity to swim. This is where I took swimming lessons and learned how to swim the proper way.

Later in my 20s, I joined the South End Rowing Club on Jefferson Street near Fisherman's Wharf. Founded in 1873, The South End Rowing Club is one of the oldest athletic clubs in the western United States. The club had handball courts, a sundeck, shower facilities, and annual swims under the Golden Gate Bridge from the San Francisco side opposite Fort Point at slack tide. We would swim to the other side near Lime Rock where we were picked up by a boat and returned to the club. I did this twice, having completed one crossing on Sunday October 24, 1954 in 37 minutes and 33 seconds. The winning time: 28 minutes and 30 seconds. The other time was 33 minutes and 4 seconds. The winning time was 28 minutes and 29 seconds.

The event planners for these swims had the tides in mind when the tides were changing from low to high or high to low, thus giving the swimmers basically slack water (no movement in either direction) for about half an hour. We boarded a Red Stack Tug at Pier 43, dove off the boat on the San Francisco side near Fort Point, and were picked up on the other side at Lime Rock.

The swims were in the early morning hours. No one wore wetsuits. When the swim had been completed we were returned to Pier 43 and then to the South End Rowing Club at approximately 11:30 am., where lunch was served, then dancing to the music of Paul Law and His Orchestra at 1:00 p.m. The presentation of trophies by Judge Walter Carpenetti took place at 3:00 p.m., and finally, dancing until 5:00 p.m. highlighted the evening, This information was obtained from the "South End Rowing Club Program of the Day." Sunday, October 24, 1954.

Alcatraz to Aquatic Park became another annual swim I completed a couple of times. Another swim was the United Crusade's Treasure Island swim – a three-quarter-mile swim from Pier 7 that ended at the isthmus that separates Treasure Island and Yerba Buena Island. The time I attempted this, diving off the pier, the current became too strong and swept most of us down in a southerly direction. We each had a shell boat assigned to us that picked us up. Only a few swimmers were able to make it to the island.

Finally, there was an annual swim from Yacht Harbor to the South End Rowing Club– a two and a quarter mile route. One year, I completed the swim in forty-six minutes. The winning time was 41 minutes and 62 seconds. Naturally, no wetsuits. The Bay's and the Ocean's temperatures are about 54 degrees, so 45 minutes without a wetsuit would cause swimmers to experience hypothermia which included shaking and being uncomfortable.

Kelly's Cove, directly below the Cliff House at Ocean Beach, became another popular hangout for surfers like myself in the 1950's and beyond. Many of us both young and older would swim without wetsuits and enjoy various other water activities such as body surfing, with and without rubber fins, and riding the waves with a four by two Hodgman – an inflated rubber mattress that we inflated with 100 pounds of air enabling us to ride a bumpy wave of any size.

My Bragg Surfboard

Other than surfing, we played "wall ball" using a small rubber hard ball similar to a handball thrown against the concave sea wall. Football and racing in the sand were another activity. We would burn a rubber tire to keep warm and surprisingly, it did not emit an odor as the smoke rose in the air. On the way to the beach, the Fat Boy Restaurant located at Lincoln Way and Lower Great Highway afforded the most delicious barbecue sandwiches and hot dogs.

An article written by Lisa Martinovic in the SF Chronicle dated February 11, 2000 and titled: "Charlie's Last Ride," describes Charlie Grimm's last ocean experience as his ashes were scattered into the ocean by his friends near Kelly's Cove. He was a humble and personable person, surfer, and a San Francisco Fireman. He was often seen riding a wave under its arc. He surfed before the era of wetsuits.

At Charlie's ceremony, the article continues, "One of the firemen came to the center of the gathering with an old-fashioned bell, the signaling device used by firefighters before the age of computers. He tapped it five times – the code of something being put out of service permanently" … He was 69 when he died of a brain tumor. <u>Copyright Permission granted.</u> Rest in Peace, Charlie.

Pictured above: 2nd row and left to right with hand raised, John Quartz, Homer Hudelson, Max Girard, and George Farnsworth. It's been so long I can't recall the other swimmers' names, although there are possible ways to retrieve them – by going to the club, for example. This picture shows us on our way from Pier 43 on the Red Stack Tug toward the San Francisco side near Fort Point to begin the swim to Lime Rock to the North side under the Golden Gate Bridge. I was in my 20s at the time.

South End Rowing Club

Boat House
Hyde and Jefferson Streets
San Francisco, Calif.

PROGRAM

25th Annual

GOLDEN GATE SWIM

Sunday, October 24, 1954

Dedicated To

ED BROWN

Athletic Director Sacramento, Elks

and

GEORGE BRADY

Boathouse Captain,
South End Rowing Club

Program of the Day

(PACIFIC STANDARD TIME)

8:00 a.m. (No later) Swimmers and pilots gather at the Clubhouse.

9:00 a.m. Coast Guard boats tow pilot boats from Aquatic Park.

9:00 a.m. Swimmers leave Pier 43

9:30 a.m. Spectator Boat leaves Pier 43½

11:30 a.m. All boats return to berths. Passengers embark for South End Rowing Club - Foot of Hyde St., Aquatic Park.

12:00 a.m. Lunch served in our kitchen.

1:00 p.m. Dance to music of Paul Law & His Orchestra

3:00 p.m. Presentation of Trophies by Judge Walter Carpenetti

3:30 p.m. Dancing until 5:00 p.m.

The Rip Tide

One time as a youth, I was caught in a rip tide at Ocean Beach and I had a very difficult time getting back to shore. Only later did I learn that if you get caught in a rip current, remain calm; backstroke is usually the best way to swim. (Rip currents are usually not very wide so no reason to panic.) Swim parallel to the shore until the rip current ends. Then swim toward the beach.

As my four children were growing up and became eligible for swimming lessons, we would sign them up yearly at South San

Francisco High School for this extremely important part of their lives. They are all good swimmers.

Also, when we lived on 48th Avenue, one of our neighbors, Gene Hokem, had a vacuum cleaner repair shop located downstairs from his upper flat. Being an avid fisherman, he belonged to the famous Tyee Club. He invited me to go fishing with him up by the Naval Air Station in Alameda when I was about 12 or 13 years old. He knew an area where the fish would feed on shrimp, making it easier to catch them. The best part of the fishing trip for me though was the grand lunch that his wife would fix—it was in a large doctor's type briefcase or what a carpetbagger with large leather handles would carry.

Mr. Hokem also raised ducks in a neighbor's backyard. We would go to the grocery store and pick up discarded lettuce leaves and feed them to the ducks. One day Mr. Hokem and his wife invited me to dinner at their residence. His wife fixed roasted duck – delicious.

My mother and father took my sister and me to the Golden Gate International Exposition, also known as the World's Fair, located on Treasure Island. We would take the streetcar to the Ferry Building and then catch a ferry boat. This occurred between 1939 and 1940.

Another trip my parents took my sister and me on was to Sacramento, California, to visit our cousin "Jack" (on my father's side) who had a pear orchard. We would take the train. His cousin, while working on the Sacramento Bridge, lost his right hand in an industrial accident, forcing him to retire. We stayed at his farm for a week or two, fishing, and if desired to see a baseball game. There were times when I went with Jack somewhere in his automobile and remember him driving his stick shift with his disability; no problem. Our cousin on occasions would send us a crate of pears through the mail to our home.

A Lynching of Two Prisoners

When I was in high school, my mother told me the story about November 9, 1933, when John Holmes and Thomas Thurmond kidnapped 22-year-old Brooke Hart, a graduate of Bellarmine College Preparatory and Santa Clara University. My brother, Wendel Rudolph, was only twelve years old at the time and living with my aunt Hilda in San Jose. She took him down to St. James Park across from the Santa Clara County Jail where a mob had entered the jail and overwhelmed the jailers and took the prisoners to be hanged, which occurred shortly thereafter, Governor James Ralph, Jr., stated he would pardon anyone convicted of the lynching.

_____

In 1950, my sister, Julia, became pregnant while a junior at Presentation High School and dropped out of school. Some months later, my dad passed away. My mother was 54 years old at that time. In those days, there were no pension plans from the SF Chronicle, therefore, my mother and I survived on some United States Savings Bonds my father had purchased. My mother also received some money from Social Security until I was 18 years old, however, I was still in high school about six months before graduation. When I reached 18 and when my mother's benefits ceased, she would not become eligible for benefits again until she became sixty-two years of age.

My mother babysat and I delivered newspapers and worked odd jobs that enabled me to graduate from Sacred Heart High School in 1952. Before I graduated, I noticed a job advertisement in the S.F. Chronicle for a clerk position with the Southern Pacific Company that paid $245.00 a month. I applied for the job and was hired which enabled me to begin employment the day after my graduation. I worked for the Southern Pacific Railway Company for six and a half years.

While employed with the Southern Pacific Railroad Company, my mother and I took two different train trips. One trip was to Vancouver, Washington, on the Shasta Daylight. It was wintertime, but a beautiful trip through the winding mountains. I remember sitting in the dining car with my mother and watching the snow falling onto the trees. Before we arrived in Vancouver, Washington, we traveled through Dunsmuir, and when we stopped for fueling, the entire area was a blanket of white snow. Nothing else was visible. Breathtaking.

The other trip we took from San Francisco was on the San Joaquin Daylight. We took the ferryboat across the SF Bay to Oakland where we caught the train to Los Angeles. We traveled over the Tehachapi Mountain Pass, a helix, like a spiral staircase. It took four engines in front of the train, one in the middle, and three engines in the back of the train to power us over the Pass. Another interesting part of this trip was the trip through Fresno where the tule fog was so dark and dense that one could hardly see more than a few feet ahead.

The below pictures depict when I was in grammar school at Holy Name both in the fourth grade and eighth grades. It shows me with another student, Gordon Hendrickson. In the 4B picture I am the second student from the left in the second row from the bottom; Gordon Hendrickson is pictured in the second row from the top at the extreme right. In the 1948 picture I am at the extreme right in the second row from the top and Gordon Hendrickson is in the top row at the extreme left in the picture.

It is interesting to note that we both entered the San Francisco Police Department, and eventually we rose to the rank of sergeant. As sergeants, we both were assigned to Park Police Station. Gordon Hendrickson was at Park Police Station upstairs when a bomb exploded (refer to the memorial in another chapter). We also both rose to the rank of lieutenant. Presently, we live close to each other and attend the San Francisco Veteran Police Officers monthly meeting in San Francisco.

In the same picture of Gordon Hendrickson and me is Jim Gentile shown in the top row second from the left. He went to Sacred Heart High School and was an all-star baseball pitcher weighing well over two hundred pounds. He played in the Major Leagues for ten years, first with the Brooklyn Dodgers at first base behind Gil Hodges, then with the Baltimore Orioles, and other major League Teams. I have a picture of him at Caesar's Restaurant on Bay Street in San Francisco a

few years ago.

Looking at the picture from left to right are Jim Gentile, me,

and Ralph Burns at a Sacred Heart High School Class Reunion

at Caesar's Restaurant in San Francisco.

Chapter 2

Growing Up

Sacred Heart High School

After graduating from Holy Name Grammar School in 1948, I attended Sacred Heart High School, a Catholic religious school led by the Christian Brothers and founded by St. John Baptist de LaSalle. When I began my freshman year in 1948, the school was old and run down. One day while I was in Chemistry class, located on the second floor of the school, I noticed that there was a small hole in the wooden flooring. Bored, I made a small ball of wadded paper and with my foot caused it to fall into the hole, which was situated between me and another student.

A few minutes later, the door opened and without any acknowledgement to the Chemistry teacher, another teacher approached the student sitting in front of me, looked down at the location of the hole, and then without warning, slapped the student across the face and then walked out of the classroom. Yes, there was corporal punishment, but it wasn't me who received the punishment.

Sacred Heart High School was located on Ellis Street between Franklin and Gough Streets, giving us easy access to public transportation. When school let out, many of us hurried down Ellis to Van Ness Avenue to transfer to other transportation. On many days, students took the Van Ness Ave Streetcar headed to Market Street. When we boarded the car, we displayed our school ticket that contained 20 rides. The conductor "punched" the ticket to validate the fare. Some of the students, including me, filled in the "punched" ticket with yellow crayon that matched the same color as the ticket, thus getting us more rides.

One day, while the car was stopped for passengers, a student took the hat off the conductor and threw it into the street. When the conductor got off to retrieve his hat, another student rang the bell to signal to the motorman that he could continue on, and this left the conductor behind. This portly conductor kept running and trying to get on the streetcar. When the streetcar reached the next block and was stopped, a student rang the bell again. This continued for several blocks until the streetcar reached Market Street and we all scattered, finally allowing the exhausted conductor back onto the streetcar.

While walking up Van Ness Avenue one morning on my way to school, I stopped and shook hands with a person in front of one of the used car lots. He was a big man with enormous hands and was impeccably dressed. We exchanged greetings and I continued on my way. Later, I learned he was Pat Valentino, a heavyweight boxer who fought for the heavyweight championship of the world at the Cow Palace. More about him later.

Horsetrader Ed

In the early 1950s, on my way up Van Ness Avenue to attend Sacred Heart High School, I would pass by Horsetrader's used car lot on the Southeast corner of Eddie and Van Ness Ave. For promotional reasons, high atop a flagpole, situated about 50 feet in the air, sat a man on a horse saddle and dressed in cowboy attire. He remained there day and night for many days. "Horsetrader Ed" Balatti was the owner. He played football three seasons for the San Francisco 49ers (1946-1948).

Despondent Man, 68, Rescued from Surf

One April Sunday when I worked at the Southern Pacific Railroad Company, another employee and I went to Ocean Beach in the early morning to fish. First, we planned our trip to the beach at low tide so we could dig for worms when the water receded. This made it easy to capture the worms as they left a small line of entry into the wet sand.

We would then use them as bait. We placed our capture into a coffee can filled with wet sand. We covered the entire fishhook with a worm that would wiggle on the hook. The fish loved the worms.

Later, as we began to fish, I noticed a small, slender, elderly man dressed in a gray wool suit about 100 feet to the south of us. This man crawled into the ocean at a depth of about a foot and a half, and then submerged his face down into the water. I dropped my fishing rod and ran down to help him. I was able to pull him out of the water to dry land. An ambulance arrived and the man was transported to Park Emergence Hospital. He was treated for immersion. I later learned his name was Chris, a 68 year-old, despondent man, attempting suicide. An Officer stated he had been despondent over an illness. He resided at a private home for the aged. A San Francisco Newspaper article described the incident.

Swim Around Alcatraz

When I joined the South End Rowing Club on Jefferson Street near Aquatic Park, in my early twenties, I met many acquaintances. Max Girard became a friend of mine. Max was a big man at two hundred pounds. He was trained by the famous Jack Lalanne at the YMCA. He was immaculate and well dressed. He had an infectious smile, a sense of humor that showed his scintillating teeth, and he wore a Stetson Hat, probably because he was bald.

Max Girard was a San Francisco Police Inspector assigned to the Robbery detail. He worked in some high profile cases - one where his partner was killed and he himself shot at, but not before killing the suspect. Max personally told me he was only a few feet away when gunfire was exchanged. The suspect's bullet went right through Max's uniform hat. Max received a gold medal; the highest medal the department awards.

One day, Max stated he intended to swim around Alcatraz from the Aquatic Park Cove—a harbor protected by a circular concrete walkway with an opening to the Bay. The back of the South End Rowing Club and the adjacent Dolphin Club afforded easy access to the cove from their clubs. Many of us members would swim around the cove for exercise. We agreed on a specific day for our swim around Alcatraz.

We planned to swim at the end of an incoming tide, then after this would be the slack tide I mentioned before, and then the beginning of the outgoing tide. This would give us the best chance of swimming around Alcatraz and returning to the cove. It should be noted that tides are influenced by the Sun, Moon and the Earth's alignment and change four times every 24 hours and 50 minutes—two high tides and two low tides.

We each had a shell boat manned by a member from the club to accompany us on our trek. When we started out and were halfway to the easterly end of Alcatraz, the shell boat accompanying me began to take on water. The rower told me he had to go back to the club; I told him I would continue on, but as Max increased his distance, I decided to return to the club alone.

Alone, and out in the middle of the Bay with only a bright yellow swimming cap, I wasn't prepared to swim by myself in the Bay as various ships travel in and out of the Bay. After a short time, a U. S. Coast Guard vessel came alongside me, threw me a nautical life ring, brought me aboard, and took me back to the club. When I got back to the club, I went up to the sun deck and saw a member looking out toward Alcatraz. I asked him what he was looking for and he said, "I think someone from the club drowned."

Max completed the swim around Alcatraz and back to the club in one hour and forty-five minutes. When he got out of the 54-degree water he was shaking uncontrollably; without a wetsuit. The famous writer for the SF Chronicle, Herb Caen, wrote an entire article about his accomplishment. Quite a feat — notwithstanding mine. Max died on Columbus Day, October 1, 2013. He was 99 years old.

The South End Rowing Club had other swims in the Bay. One such swim was from Alcatraz to the entrance of the South End Rowing Club. This two-mile plus trek takes about 35 minutes for most swimmers, including me. Swimmers would be taken out to Alcatraz on a boat a certain distance away from the buoys that circled the island, and would dive off the boat.

When Alcatraz had federal prisoners, armed guards would protect the island from anyone coming within proximity of the buoys. On some high tides with the water running in or out of the Bay, buoy markers would almost be horizontal to the water. Intriguing, to say the least.

Chapter 3

The San Francisco Police Journey

1958- 1988

I entered the SF Police Department on October 22, 1958 and completed a three and half month academy program at their facility located in the outer Richmond District on Fulton Street on the South Side between 36th and 37th Street.

After successfully completing the written examination for the San Francisco Police Department, I took a physical agility test, and had a physical examination and background check. Having passed these requirements, I entered the police academy on October 22, 1958. I was one of over seventy recruits. I spent the next three and a half months in the police academy.

While still in the academy, another recruit and I were chosen to observe if alcohol was consumed on the premises at the Broken Drum Tavern after 2:00 a.m., in violation of the Alcohol Tobacco and Firearms Code. The Broken Drum was located on Market Street on the southeast corner near the Ferry Building. We were probably chosen for this assignment because of our youthful appearance.

The other officer and I arrived after 2:00 a.m. to observe if any violations occurred. To our surprise, there were only male customers, many of them were dancing and even kissing each other. A female cocktail waitress was serving drinks. The drinks were served in coffee cups. A piano player provided the entertainment. Being only 24 years old, this was my first experience of interaction with gay men. For me, it was quite an experience because I was sheltered as a youth in my upbringing.

While I was in the police academy, my sister, Julia, passed away at the age of 26 from Hodgkin's disease. Her husband, George, was now widowed with four young children. He was forced to put his children in foster care. Julia is buried in Holy Cross Cemetery; may she rest in peace.

Following completion of the 86th recruit class, over seventy recruits were sworn in to the SFPD by Chief Thomas Cahill at the Veterans' Memorial Building located on Van Ness Avenue in San Francisco. Chief Cahill was a no-nonsense former homicide inspector, who had flaming red hair, an intimidating presence, and a strong Irish brogue.

After being sworn in, we were advised to borrow $500.00 from the SF Police Credit Union that was located near the police horse stables and near Park Police Station. A disabled police wagon driver in a wheelchair issued a check in the amount of $500.00 and then he cashed the check—from a single cash drawer—so we could purchase a uniform - two shirts, hat, belt, tie, shoes - and an off-duty weapon if so desired. I purchased the above items and had approximately $200.00 left. Incidentally, this was early in the beginning of the SF Police Credit Union, now over a billion-dollar institution.

Potrero and Mission Stations

Initially I was assigned to Potrero Station, located on Potrero Street across from the American Can Company. I was assigned administrative duties inside the station (answering phone calls). Other duties were "wagon duty" or transporting prisoners, radio car assignments that required responding to calls, and being proactive by making arrests.

One of my first assignments was with wagon duty that took the driver and me into the projects in Hunters Point to pick up a prisoner. After picking up the prisoner, I went to the back of the open-ended wagon (no door) and held onto the two handles attached to the wagon to guard and keep the prisoner from escaping. Soon after, a barrage of rocks were hitting the patrol wagon. Luckily, I didn't get hit. Later, after one year, I was transferred to Northern Police Station performing the same duties as I had at Potrero Station, now known as Bayview Station.

Still, another year later, I was transferred to Mission Police Station on Valencia Street. It was common to be transferred three times after graduating from the Police Academy to gain a different perspective among the different districts within the city.

The Social Clubs

Being single in the 1950s, I often went to dances that were mostly with four-piece bands. St. James had a Catholic social club that held dances at Nick's Restaurant in Pacifica. In fact, Nick's still has dancing to live music today. Another social club that held dances for Catholic single people was held at a social room on the grounds of Old St. Mary's Church located at California and Grant Streets.

Still another was at the Sir Francis Drake Hotel located on Powell Street in Union Square. On one of the top floors of the hotel was a ballroom and a bar. Ladies would sit on chairs on the edge of the ballroom and men would approach them and see if they would accept a dance. Not all would. Finally, there was a large ballroom with an orchestra that held dances, located on the southwest corner of Market and South Van Ness Avenue.

The Traffic Bureau

While at Mission Station, I requested to be transferred to the Traffic Bureau, namely, two-wheel motorcycle duty, also known as the "Solos." After three years in the SF Police Department, I was transferred to the Traffic Bureau. Training lasted three months with the motorcycle unit. Additional pay was awarded — approximately 5%.

If an officer lived in the City, that officer could take the motorcycle home. Since I lived on 26th Street, and then later on Brunswick Street, I could take my bike home. There was camaraderie among the seventy or so officers assigned to the unit. In fact, there were frequent social gatherings with dinner and dancing with our wives or girlfriends.

When I joined the SF Police Department in 1958, there were eight district police stations throughout the city (now there are 10) that had boundaries for radio cars and for foot beat assignments. If an officer was assigned to a radio car, that office would handle assignments from radio headquarters within those boundaries or sectors, as they were called.

When busy, a radio car from another sector would be dispatched to handle an assignment out of his or her sector. It was not uncommon for other officers to ask why they were out of their sector. This was somewhat confining, as opposed to the Traffic Bureau, where a call to investigate a traffic collision could be anywhere in the city. Solos had a much larger geographical area within which to enforce traffic violations or investigate accidents. Complete autonomy.

In addition, the Solos were required to escort funerals to different cemeteries for interment, even out of the city limits. such as Holy Cross Cemetery. On other occasions, we would provide traffic security for dignitaries, politicians, and foreign diplomats, and even famous entertainers. An example was when Prince Charles came to visit San Francisco. He was given a motorcycle escort from San Francisco International Airport, then throughout his stay in San Francisco. Before he left the city, the entire complement of our unit (12 officers) met in the basement of the Fairmont Hotel. We were dressed in our Class A Uniforms. This was a ¾ length uniform coat with a belt that went over the coat in a diagonal position and then around the waist. The Prince addressed each officer. He wore a dark, impeccable pinstripe suit. As he extended his hand to me, I made it a point to mention how it was such a special honor to meet him and to escort him on this special visit to San Francisco. We gave him a motorcycle helmet as a gift, and escorted him back to the airport. We also escorted Pope John Paul II, now declared a saint by the Catholic Church, throughout the city. These occurrences gave us a special appreciation for our job.

I also met the Apollo 8 astronauts, Frank Borman, Jim Lovell, and William Anders, who came to the city; we also escorted them. This gave me an opportunity to get their autographs. I requested they write something to our oldest son, Albert; he was 6 years old at the time. They honored my request and all three signed a short greeting. Albert still has this treasure. Apollo 8 was the first spacecraft to orbit the moon. It orbited ten times in a period of seven days on December 21, 1968.

Finally, an escort was provided for a famous rock band in San Francisco and when they were escorted to the Sir Francis Drake Hotel on Powell Street our Solo Motorcycle unit made a pathway for them to enter the hotel. This was because a crowd gathered and began screaming as the band was entering the hotel, but before escaping from the crowd a person reached over the shoulder of a police officer, grabbed one of the entertainers by his head, and removed a lock of his hair.

It's ironic that after I was promoted to Lieutenant and assigned to Potrero Station some twenty-seven years later, on December 4, 1985, I would be the first police officer to arrive at a stabbing on 25th Street between Third Street and Texas Streets. The house was located on a steep hill. The residence had a garage that was situated in front of the property and separated from the house. A woman approximately 28 years old was entering her residence when she was attacked. Her home was burglarized; she was raped, robbed and murdered.

When I arrived on the scene the victim, naked, with stab wounds on her left side, was deceased. I preserved the crime scene and called for an ambulance, homicide unit, coroner, and crime scene investigators.

The coroner is the person in charge of the crime scene until turned over to the homicide unit. A knife was found in front of the house, obviously the murder weapon. I remained at the scene for a while and observed that the crime scene investigators sprayed some type of sticky liquid onto the walls, tables, and the telephone.

During this time, high intensity lamps were used to display fingerprints. These would be gathered for evidence. No suspects were arrested. Sometime later, I went to the homicide detail to see if anyone had been arrested with negative results. A homicide inspector informed me that a credit card of the victim was found in an elevator in the Potrero Hill Projects.

Twenty-two years later, after I arrived home from playing golf, Gloria informed me that a homicide inspector asked me to contact him. When I got in touch with him, they identified the killer through his DNA and that I might be called to the jury trial. I was not summoned to a trial. After a second trial, the killer was found guilty and given a life sentence without the possibility of parole.

Northern and Mission Police Stations

In 1959, I was assigned to Northern Police Station performing the same duties as I performed at Potrero Station. In 1961, I was transferred to Mission Station on Valencia Street. In October of 1961, after a suspect made two unsuccessful attempts on a person's life at a residence on 20th Street, I was chosen to prevent another incident. A lieutenant, in consultation with a sergeant, recommended that I be placed in the residence. In addition to my service revolver, I was to be armed with a shotgun.

After the residents were notified that I would be situated in their residence, I entered the building. There were about 20 stairs to the top of the building. I spoke to a woman who lived there and informed her that if anyone rang the doorbell, I would open the door with the door lever handle that was located at the top of the stairs. If I observed a suspect, I informed her to call the police and tell them that it was an emergency and that a police officer needed immediate help.

After some time, I took off my uniform coat and waited for any intrusion. The shotgun was loaded, but no round chambered. It wasn't long before the doorbell rang. I opened the door by pulling the handle located on the side of the wall and when the person downstairs observed me, he immediately took off running. I discarded the shotgun, ran down the stairs and chased the suspect about a quarter of a block to a vehicle located on the west side of Folsom Street near 20th Street. The vehicle driver's window was rolled down, so I placed my handgun to his temple and ordered him out of the car. I handcuffed him and recovered a handgun on the driver's side of the floorboard area. I heard numerous sirens and then the approaching police cars that arrived at the scene.

I received a second grade meritorious award, the second highest award that the SFPD issues. About six months later, a trial was held and the suspect was found guilty and sent to a state penitentiary.

On November 27, 1964, when I was with the Solos, there was an evening holdup at 14th and Valencia streets on the southwest corner. Numerous police units responded, however, the suspects escaped. Sometime later and after the police units left the scene, I noticed a man standing on the southeast corner of Valencia and 14th St., so I approached him and asked him if he had seen anything. He stated, "I don't want my name known." I informed him not to worry and that is when he told me where the suspects had fled.

A police academy classmate of mine, Frank McNitt, also on a two-wheel motorcycle, responded to the crime scene. I informed him of what I knew, so we went to the residence where the suspects had fled. After ringing the doorbell to the upstairs flat, the door opened and a youth upon seeing us, ran downstairs to the backyard area with us in pursuit.

We captured him and had him transported to Mission Station where we interrogated him. After some time, we convinced him that the best thing was to tell the truth. He told us where the other two of his friends lived. We went to their residences, placed them under arrest, and had them processed and taken to the youth guidance center. It was about 4 a.m. when we were able to complete our work and go home.

Frank McNitt and I both lived in San Francisco, so we were able to take our SF Police motorcycles home. Shortly after my oldest daughter, Cathy, was born, while Frank and I were on duty, we went to my house on Brunswick Street to visit my newborn daughter. After that we became good friends. Later, he invited me and my wife to stay with him and his wife at his house in Lake Tahoe. He left his two young children with his parents. Gloria and I had other obligations and we were unable to go to his cabin at this time.

Frank and his wife took the trip to Lake Tahoe anyway, but they did not come home on their designated day. Because of this, Frank's parents had the CHP investigate their well-being. The CHP discovered Frank and his wife in their cabin both asphyxiated from carbon monoxide. Frank's mother and father, I believe, were both in their 60s and took care of the children. Rest in peace to you and your wife, Frank.

A Toy Gun

While in the SF Police Academy in 1958, we learned among other things that before going on an assignment in a radio car we should search the police vehicle for contraband and/ or weapons, even though this was the responsibility of the last police officer using the vehicle. After being assigned to Potrero Police Station—my first station and my first radio car assignment—I located a toy gun under the back seat of the police vehicle. It was strikingly similar to a four-inch S&W revolver. Looking into the barrel of the toy gun one could see that silver like bullets were placed into the cylinder. I booked the contraband as property for identification in case this toy weapon could be connected to a crime.

This toy gun was probably used or would be used in some sort of crime. One could even imagine that if this was a real weapon it could have caused an officer his life. The person that was placed in the rear seat of the patrol car by an officer was not searched properly. Hard to believe.

Shark Attack

In all the years swimming at Ocean Beach, I can recall only one shark attack. It occurred on Thursday May 7th, 1959 at Baker Beach. A couple were out in shallow water located just below the Presidio near the Golden Gate Bridge, when a great white shark attacked the upper part of the man's body and arm.

The woman, putting herself in harm's way, embraced him, and assisted him back to shore. People on the beach noticed this daring rescue. Once on the beach, the woman gathered some ocean water in her cupped hands and poured the water over his body and baptized him "In the Name of the Father, and of the Son, and of the Holy Spirit." Then she had him say an Act of Contrition. He died shortly thereafter.

Die by the Sword

In 1954, while Frances J. Ahern was the Chief of Police in San Francisco, a brutal murder took place. The victim, 71, was murdered in an antique shop on Valencia Street. Chief Ahern vowed to appoint any police officer to the bureau of inspectors, a very sought after assignment, the following day if that person arrested this killer who stabbed, beat, and burned the victim with cigarettes in an apparent attempt to learn where money or other valuables were hidden.

Bloody fingerprints and a sword with blood on it were some of the damning evidence found at the murder scene. A suspect, Kidd, was identified. A witness stated to police that he and his friend would often go drinking on Valencia Street. In addition, a bartender from the Pink Horse Tavern located on the same street as the one where the victim was murdered stated that the suspect had been in his tavern the day of the murder. After the murder, the suspect traveled to Valparaiso, Indiana; he stated to police he went there to find work. He was subsequently brought back from Indiana in 1960 to face trial for murder. On October 18, 1962, Kidd was found guilty of first degree murder and sentenced to death.

On November 2, 1961, the suspect was granted a new trial based on the impeachment of the coroner's testimony. In April 1962, the suspect was granted a new trial based on improper instructions to the jury. Even though it has been sixty years since the murder of the victim I still remember some facts regarding this case.

For example, I remember a picture of a woman on the front page of the SF Chronicle who I thought was his mother, stating she would offer free cleaning services for an extended time if someone would defend her son. Vincent Hallinan, a famous trial attorney, accepted the offer; pro bono to defend Kidd. Educated in S.F. at St. Ignatius High School and USF, Hallinan had a striking appearance and strong features.

I happened to be at the Hall of Justice on another trial in 1962. After my case ended, I entered the courtroom where Kidd was on trial. This trial, to say the least, was filled with interesting witnesses and challenges.

Witnesses were put on the "hot seat" in cross examination. However, one witness was dismissed rather quickly. He was Ralph McDonald, a S.F. Homicide Detective. I remember Vincent Hallinan when addressing McDonald on the stand asked him, "You're only a patrolman, isn't that right?" Inspector McDonald stated, "No, I'm a sergeant."

With his double-breasted blue suit unbuttoned and his legs crossed in such a relaxed position, he was only asked a few more questions and then excused from the witness stand. I remember another incident at this trial when a pathologist, Dr. Moon, stated that the cause of death was a sword driven into the upper part of the victim's body. The trial ended with the suspect being acquitted and released in July 1962.

149 Times

It should be noted that at the district stations besides radio car and foot patrol assignments, there are wagon duties that respond to intoxicated subjects and other prisoners that need to be brought back to the district stations for booking and then placed in the holding cell until they are transported to the City Prison at the Hall of Justice.

Some district stations at the beginning of watch make a "roundup" of intoxicated persons. On some occasions this does not preclude a person from being transported in a radio car back to the district station or transported to the City Prison. At the District Stations they are to be held no more than four hours before being transported to the Hall of Justice.

Sometime in December of 1961, I was working out of Mission Police Station in a patrol car with another officer and was assigned to respond to 24th and Hampshire Streets regarding a drunken person.

Upon our arrival, we observed a man, obviously intoxicated and acting irrationally. We decided to transport him to the Hall of Justice. While he was being transported to the Hall of Justice for booking he thought that rats were crawling on him and then he pointed to a non-existent car he said was following the paddy wagon. To me, this was a sign of delirium tremens - alcohol withdrawal. We later learned that this man had been arrested one hundred and forty-nine times for public intoxication. We drove him to the Hall of Justice for processing. We later learned that he would challenge the law and the law would be ruled unconstitutional because of its vagueness.

Earlier in 1961, while stationed at Northern Police Station and walking a beat with a seasoned police officer on Fillmore Street, I entered a pool hall and when the veteran police officer noticed a particular person he summoned him and said, "I told you not to come here." At this time there was a vagrancy law and more noteworthy a "thousand dollar vag (vagrant)." These laws made it a crime to wander from place to place without visible means of support. He was placed under arrest and transported to Northern Police Station via a

wagon.

Chapter 4

The Cliff House

The Cliff House as of December 31, 2020 closed its doors for good as COVID-19 took its toll on restaurants (in addition to other issues with the National Parks Service as of January 2021). The Cliff House, established in 1863, is a landmark and part of the Golden Gate National Recreation Area, operated by the National Park Service. It has delighted many tourists as well as locals. People from all over the world would come to enjoy the food and the beautiful scenery.

Gloria and other family members enjoyed many lunches in the upper part of the restaurant in the Cliff House. The ascent from Kelly's Cove to the Cliff House is about 1,000 feet, which gives outstanding views of the vast Pacific Ocean and surrounding areas like the Marin Headlands. Even today, after sixty-two years when I first met Gloria near the Cliff House, we still come into San Francisco to buy the best made Oatmeal Raisin Cookies at Boudin Bakery at their Tenth and Geary Boulevard location. Boudin Bakery was established in San Francisco in the year 1849 and is said to be the oldest continually operating business in The City.

The Tenth Avenue location is also a Historical Landmark of over one hundred years constructed in 1906 after the San Francisco Earthquake. It is designated as a Historical Business by the California Historical Society. A plaque is situated to the left of the building's entrance on the outer wall. A few feet to the right of the entrance to the bakery are presently eighteen names of past and present workers' footprints embedded in the sidewalk. Boudin presently has other locations in the Bay Area.

On occasion, we would also purchase the Italian Classic Sandwich with salami, mortadella, provolone cheese, lettuce, Dijon, and mayo, on a sourdough baguette. In addition, we also purchase the Rustic Tomato Soup. With these items we would bring along potato chips and a can of ginger ale to share. After purchasing these items, we would drive down to the Cliff House, find a parking space overlooking the ocean, and watch the waves breaking and rolling into the beach. Watching the windsurfers and surfboard riders was an enjoyable way to have lunch.

Situated downstairs in the Cliff House was another eating area – a more formal dining area. In the upper restaurant and bar, food was served with warm "popovers" – so named because the air beaten into the eggs and the steam from the wet butter caused the pastry to puff up and pop over the baking tin. The popovers were served before the entree and were brought to the booth in a small bread basket covered with a cloth napkin. They were hot or at least warm, and we could choose to put butter, marmalade, or strawberry preserves on the inside of the popover. These were really delicious, especially with a hot cup of coffee. I remember my mother making popovers for us.

Numerous framed photos of celebrities and movie stars with their signatures hung from the walls by the booths for the customer's viewing—I would often ask friends: "Who did you sit next to? Bing Crosby, Loretta Young, Spencer Tracy, Gary Grant, Fred MacMurray?"

Looking directly out of the large windows one could view Seal Rock, which is the largest of several rocks. In the middle of this large rock is a fjord, which is in a southerly to northerly direction. I know, because on one occasion I swam out opposite this rock within a few feet to the south to view it. Seals used to gather on the rock. Various birds, like seagulls or pelicans, could be seen gliding by the windows. Groups of pelicans with their large beaks and graceful gliding flight are sometimes very close to the water looking for their prey and on other occasions would dive from high altitudes, like a dive-bomber, to catch their prey. A truly beautiful bird.

Patrons could also view large ships entering through the channels of the Bay. Many of these ships had to wait for low tides so as to go safely under the Golden Gate Bridge. Ships inspected by the US Coast Guard were then escorted into the Bay by San Francisco Bar Pilots. The Bar Pilots Association was created in 1850. Their annual salary (at this writing) is approximately one half million dollars. Getting hired as a Bar Pilot is difficult as my departed friend, Dave Seyler, informed me. Nepotism?

Especially in the early part of the year, while Gloria and I were having lunch in the upper restaurant, we would have a chance to watch gray whales dive beneath the waters in search of food and after several submerged minutes, rise up through the water and blow a watery mist through their blowhole. This is the time of the year they migrate to the warm waters of Baja California to give birth to their young. Later they would return to Alaska with their young. Humpback whales and other species also travel these waters. Binoculars would give a person a better view watching these huge mammals navigate the waters

Love at First Sight

I met Gloria Gallegos, just 20 years old, at Kelly's Cove, which is just down the hill from the Cliff House. I "hung out" at Kelly's Cove as I surfed and played various sports with other surfers at the beach. Gloria's parents, Al and Loretta Gallegos, owned Estrada's Spanish Kitchen in Colma on Old Mission Road; it was an old roadhouse and a historical landmark over one hundred years old. Other relatives owned similar restaurants in Fresno and Visalia California.

A year later we were married at Holy Angels Catholic Church in Daly City on San Pedro Road. Father Long married us. He was a former Lt. Commander in the U.S Navy. We had a large reception in Westlake after the wedding with many ice carvings displayed and food prepared by family members from the other restaurants in Fresno and Visalia. Live music was also provided.

Estrada's Spanish Kitchen served "Early California Cooking." One of the best food items was the "Hot Salad." Ingredients were a cooked tortilla covered with refried beans and chorizo. It was then placed on a thick iron plate for about fifteen minutes in an oven at 450 degrees. Taken out of the oven the tostada would be placed on another plate and a healthy portion of shredded lettuce would be placed on top of the tostada. Next, a jar with a perforated top containing oil, vinegar, and whole garlic clove would be poured over the tostado causing a sizzling warm vapor to rise from the tostada. Red-hot sauce and a few black olives would be placed on top of the lettuce; my favorite.

On one occasion, my daughter, Laurie, and her eight-year-old daughter, Alyssa, met us at the "Kitchen" for dinner. We sat together in a booth and ordered our dinner and when our food arrived and was placed on the table, Alyssa noticed my Hot Salad. Alyssa then said, "I want to sit next to Papa" We both enjoyed the Hot Salad.

Other favorite foods on the menu were chili relleno, fried chicken, macaroni in a delicious roux, chili con carne, combination plates with refried beans and enchiladas, and beef, chicken, and cheese tamales. A bar also afforded cocktails and beer. Many evenings, customers would wait outside for a table inside the restaurant. The restaurant did not open until 5:00 o'clock. When the restaurant was inspected for inspection by the San Mateo County Health Environmental Services it always received high marks, especially for cleanliness; the written inspection was posted for viewing in the restaurant.

On our honeymoon, Gloria and I traveled to the Estrada's restaurant in Visalia and visited with Gloria's relatives, and naturally, had dinner there. We also went to Morro Bay where we stayed at a house owned by Gloria's relatives. Gloria had two sisters, Barbara and Margaret; Margaret the younger of the two.

Our first residence was on 26th Street between Church and Dolores in San Francisco, and then we moved to a house on Brunswick Street, also in SF. Later, in 1966 we bought a house in South SF where we presently live. We have four children: two boys, and two girls. They all attended Catholic Schools: St. Veronica Grammar School, Mercy High School, Junipero Serra High School, and St. Ignatius High School. Three of our children are teachers and one is in sales and is an accomplished musician. Presently, we have eight grandchildren and one great grandchild.

Because of the demands of the restaurant business, my wife, while also raising our four children, would spend many hours working at Estrada's. She would often come home late but would always prepare our kids' lunches and press their uniforms before going to bed. Our home was always immaculate thanks to her. I took evening classes at Skyline College earning an Associate in Arts Degree in May of 2002 in the Administration of Justice. With work and family demands, it took me almost nine years to receive my degree.

When our children were growing up, we often traveled to Konocti Resort in Clearlake, California. This was the Local 38 Plumbers' Resort. It had several swimming pools, some with diving boards, pee wee golf, a teen center, fishing from the piers, a restaurant, and a coffee shop. Since access to the resort had security, parents did not have to worry about their children.

Gloria and I often rented an apartment that had a barbeque. Close by was the Buckingham Golf Course where I often played. It was a nine-hole circular course around a lake; it was played from different tee positions for the second group of nine holes. This made the experience feel as if a person were playing a regular eighteen-hole course.

Our children grew up in the family restaurant business and we never went hungry, thanks to Gloria's parents. My mother never went hungry either. Gloria and I continued to support my mother after our marriage. On one occasion before our marriage, Gloria's mother stated, "You know Homer has his mother to support." Gloria married me knowing that I had the responsibility to support my mother. My mother lived by herself in Colma for a while, then with her son, Wendel, in San Jose. We supported my mother for another 24 years.

On Thanksgiving Day, my mother took the Greyhound Bus into San Francisco where Gloria and I picked her up at the Seventh Street Station near Market Street and brought her to Estrada's for dinner. Later, after dinner, we drove her back to the Greyhound Depot for her return to San Jose.

Later, my mother lived by herself in San Jose until she was diagnosed with dementia and accepted into Casa Olga, a senior living community in Palo Alto. Casa Olga was a beautiful place for senior residents, with restaurants, shopping availability, and a beauty salon across the street. After a few years, well into her eighties, she needed more advanced care and entered a convalescent hospital in San Jose.

When we visited her there, we would ask her if she wanted something from Dairy Queen (across the street) and she would reply, "If you please." Her reply came from her childhood as she and her sister while at the dinner table would remain silent until spoken to and speak only if they were offered additional servings of food. She carried it into her adult life.

Recently I read some information about St. Teresa Benedicta of the Cross (Edith Stein). She believed that life has a complete and coherent meaning in God's eyes. This statement resonates with me today in a profound way because at the time of my father's death when I was sixteen, I never worried about how the situation might unfold with my mother. As Christ hung on the cross, he told John, "Behold thy Mother." Then to Mary, "Behold thy Son." From that moment on, John took Our Lord's Mother into His home.

St. Teresa of Benedicta, a former Jewish Philosopher who later became a Carmelite Catholic Nun, died at the age of 50 in the Auschwitz-Birkenau Concentration Camp in Poland. My mother passed away at eighty-seven and is buried in San Jose's Oak Hill Cemetery along with her son who is buried in the Veterans' section. Rest in peace.

———

My father-in-law, Albert Gallegos, served his country in World War II, receiving the Purple Heart. He purchased a home on the 17 Mile Drive in Pebble Beach from Frankie Albert, the noted quarterback for the SF Forty-Niners. We spent many memorable occasions there with our family.

Because the home was located on 17 Mile Drive and had very little traffic, it was safe for our children to play in front of the house.

For example, they had many fun filled hours playing Frisbee. This house was only two short blocks from the ocean and afforded us access to the ocean and pathways along the beach. Albert Gallegos knew a friend of his that lived nearby and belonged to the Monterey Peninsula Golf Course, so we were able to play at the course several times.

Later, Albert and Loretta sold their restaurant and moved to Oakmont, a retirement community located in Santa Rosa and then moved to San Jose. Finally, they moved to a mobile home park in Hayward. This move enabled them to be nearer family members in their later years. They both passed away in their eighties. Rest in peace.

Milestones

In 2010, Gloria discovered bruising throughout her body. We went to our family doctor who referred us to a specialist who sent Gloria to Seton Hospital to receive platelets—cell fragments in the blood that form clots and stop or prevent bleeding; they are normally made in our bone marrow.

After receiving platelets every other day, the doctor suggested that she go to either Stanford or UCSF for special treatment that would not be available anywhere else; we chose UCSF. UCSF, one of the finest hospitals in the world; it features as a hierarchy, which at the top are PHD doctors, research, doctors, nurse practitioners, nurses, etc. At UCSF she was diagnosed with aplastic anemia; a rare condition in which the body stops producing enough new blood cells.

One evening after consultation with her doctor at UCSF, it was decided that she should try a special treatment. It was the evening before the treatment that she collapsed, fortunately she fell in front of a doctor who injected her with a medicine in her carotid artery as her kidneys were shutting down. It was just in time as she was taken to the Critical Care Unit for treatment and observation.

It was there that she received the Last Rites of the Catholic Church. A few days later, her condition improved enough that she was transferred to a ward in the hospital. I was there when three doctors entered the room and stated, "We don't see this turn around very often." She began many regular treatments over the years and her condition has stabilized. It has been over 10 years; a miracle!

On May 1, 2021, Gloria and I celebrated our 60th wedding anniversary at the Basque Cultural Center in South San Francisco on Railroad Avenue with 28 family members and friends. Some family and friends were unable to come to the anniversary due to COVID-19 and other issues. Some special friends included Hazel, who was Gloria's beautician for over 49 years, and Hazel's husband, Chris. Another longtime friend, Jerome Cassidy and his wife, Judy, were in attendance. I worked with Jerome in the SF Police Department for over 25 years. I played golf in his golf club, and as friends we also socialized.

The Basque Cultural Center has an enjoyable atmosphere. Guests and family members enjoyed sumptuous cuisine — salad, salmon, chicken, rice and vegetables, and a spectacular strawberry shortcake from Mazzetti's Bakery, a local Pacifica favorite. Our favorite son-in-law (and only one) brought sparkling wine for all to share. Cathy and Laurie, our two daughters, presented a video showcasing our sixty years together. Gloria, and I felt blessed and honored at our milestone celebration.

Chapter 5

Sixteen Years

Before my transfer to the Traffic Bureau, someone from the bureau informed me that since I only weighed 165 pounds, I should gain more weight. After speaking to other police officers, some suggested that I go to Alex's Gym located on the northeast corner of Mission and Russia Streets.

I met Alex and he informed me that if I lifted weights three times a week for approximately six months, I could weigh up to 175 pounds. There were quite a few San Francisco Police Officers who worked out at this particular gym. I did gain the sought-after weight and after another six months, squatted with a best of 300 pounds with "free weights" — not attached to a wall device — and bench pressed a best of 260 pounds. I ultimately weighed 185 pounds and remained at that weight for sixteen years.

While I was at the gym one day, I stepped out of the front door just to take a break when I observed a tall skinny man standing next to the parking meter with the flap down, exposing money that would be collected. I asked him what he was doing and at that moment with a clenched fist he threw something across the street when I grabbed him.

After a short struggle, I brought him into the gym and sat him down on a bench surrounded by some off-duty police officers. He sat quietly until the patrol wagon from Ingleside Station arrived and he was transported to booking for petty theft. I looked all around for a key to the parking meter, but was unable to find it. The case was dismissed.

The suspect and I crossed paths two more times - once for a loud muffler violation where he had warrants for his arrest. I arrested him and booked a bag of coins as evidence from his vehicle. In court, he asked for this money to be returned. Finally, on a Sunday morning I responded to an accident where he rear-ended a Muni Trolley Car on Mission Street near 24th Streets. I booked him for being under the influence of drugs. He stated, "Hudelson, you're after me."

Timothy L. Silva

Winter 1963-1964

After issuing a traffic citation near Army and Pennsylvania Streets while assigned two-wheel motorcycle duty on a sunny afternoon, I noticed a person hitchhiking on the North side of Army Street about fifty yards East of where I had issued the traffic citation. When I started to leave the area, I decided that I should speak to the hitchhiker and advise him about the California Vehicle Code violation.

When I approached him and asked him for his identification, he refused. I requested a back-up and Officer Richard Abbey from Potrero Station responded. Again, I asked the hitchhiker for his identification and again he refused, using foul language. When Officer Abbey and I attempted to place handcuffs on his wrists he resisted, but we succeeded and transported him to Potrero Station. The hitchhiker's name was Timothy L. Silva.

I went to court the next day, and before Judge Lenore Underwood, who admonished Silva and said, "The next time a police officer tells you to do something, do it." Silva stated that he didn't think this was against the law. He was given probation. Later in the day, Officer Richard Abbey called me and informed me that he had fractured his thumb during the arrest. I told him I was sorry and he said, "No, I'm going to be off work for six weeks."

On the night of January 6, 1964, a few months after arresting the hitchhiker, I picked up a newspaper and with Timothy L. Silva's picture on the front page of the newspaper described him as having shot and killed a Broadmoor Police Officer, Charles E. Manning. Silva was subsequently found guilty and sent to prison.

It Wasn't Worth It

1960s

While patrolling on a sunny afternoon and performing traffic enforcement duties, I pulled over a motorist for a traffic violation. After the vehicle came to a complete stop, I approached the driver's side of the vehicle. However, before I got to the vehicle the driver exited the car and said, "What did I do, what did I do?" The driver was a young female, probably in her twenties wearing a blue blouse and light brown capris. I informed her of the violation.

She was visibly shaken, and highly upset. She displayed her driver's license. I retrieved my citation book from a holder attached to the motorcycle to issue a citation for the traffic violation. Her driver's license was up to date with no restrictions. As I began to write the citation, I noticed that she had urinated in her clothing. I returned her driver's license to her and informed her that I was not going to issue her a citation. I further informed her to drive more carefully and that I was going to leave the area and before she drove away, she should, for a couple of moments, try to compose herself.

I was concerned that if I had "tagged" her she could possibly get into a traffic accident and injure herself or someone else. It wasn't worth it. It just wasn't worth it.

A Cable Car Dispute

It was in early February, 1965, in the early afternoon while on motorcycle patrol, I was notified over the police radio of a dispute with a passenger on a Cable Car at the Cable Car Turnaround located at Market and Powell Streets.

I responded to the location and met two other San Francisco Police Officers at this location: Charles Bates and Sergeant Robert McKee. There were several Cable Cars backed up and many upset passengers waiting to travel North up Powell Street toward Nob Hill to their destinations.

Mona Hutchin, 19, was standing on the outside steps of a Cable Car with a tight grip on the handrail. Cable Car employees pleaded with her to step inside, explaining to her that only men were allowed to stand on the outside steps because of safety concerns, and this was the policy of the San Francisco Municipal Railway. Miss Hutchin stated that women should have the same rights as men, and this was an asinine law. Sergeant McKee, Officer Bates, and I tried to persuade her to step inside the Cable Car, but to no avail.

Sergeant McKee, Officer Bates, and I decided to remove Miss Hutchin from the Cable Car. We gently removed her hands from the handrail but not without her resistance. We transported her to the Hall of Justice, located on Bryant Street. It was there that she expressed her reasoning and was released. To say the least, where laws and policies meet head-on, common sense should prevail.

Armed Robbery

April 1967

On April 10, 1967, Officer Warren McCormack and I were assigned to a radio car for traffic enforcement due to inclement weather conditions, making it hazardous for motorcycle duty. In the early afternoon, a radio call informed police units of an armed robbery at 24th and Taraval Streets and that a Cadillac fled the scene. Further information broadcasted stated that there were two suspects, one wearing a green sweater.

I suggested that we go to the Lower Great Highway and see if this would possibly be their escape route. Officer McCormack agreed. Since I was the driver, I positioned the radio car on the Lower Great

Highway a few feet from Lincoln Way facing north. After some time, I observed an older 1954 Brown 4-door Cadillac visible in the rear view mirror coming into view in a westerly direction on Judah Street approaching the Lower Great Highway. When I was young, I always had an interest in the year and make of automobiles.

I made a U-turn and drove to Judah Street, eventually approaching this vehicle from the rear. I put on the red lights of the patrol vehicle and pulled them over. I exited the radio car and approached the vehicle on the passenger side and noticed that neither of the two male occupants was wearing a green sweater. However, after I got closer to the vehicle I observed a green sweater under the passenger seat. I signaled to Officer McCormack. Both men were ordered out of the car and handcuffed. I discovered a handgun and it was confiscated. Both men were placed under arrest.

In court, both men were convicted and sentenced to six months in San Bruno County Jail, perhaps a lesser sentence meted out because their weapon was not operational. Officer McCormack and I each received a 3rd Grade Meritorious.

San Francisco State Demonstrations

1968

The Third World Liberation Front (TWLF) initiated a response to the lack of diversity in the college systems in California in 1968 along with the Black Student Union. Other issues were highlighted like protests against the Vietnam War. So, in 1968 at SF State College, presently SF State University, began a lengthy strike and demonstrations for these reforms. The San Francisco Police Department was assigned to monitor and enforce the law during these demonstrations. I was a part of this assignment.

We were assigned to the immediate area near the university. Another motorcycle unit, "Hondas," were sequestered inside the police range at Lake Merced so as to make a rapid response to the college when necessary. At one point during the strike, while monitoring a group of students near the entrance of the college, students threw rocks at us from the area of the street car tracks on 19th Avenue, opposite the university. Thankfully no one got hurt.

One day when I was on the grounds of the college, President S.I. Hayakawa had an altercation with some students that were using a truck with loud speakers. President Hayakawa confronted these students and the altercation ensued. This altercation ended without any injuries to my knowledge. Newspapers wrote lengthy articles about this confrontation.

On March 20, 1969, an agreement was reached and the strike officially ended but not before lengthy negotiations. The Administration retained control of hiring and admission and the creation of Ethnic Studies.

The San Francisco State demonstrations still resonate with me even though more than fifty years have passed. Gloria and I attended the graduation of our oldest daughter, Cathy, in 1985 at the university receiving her Bachelor of Arts in Liberal Studies. Later in 1986 she would receive a Teaching Credential in multiple subjects. Presently she is still teaching at a middle school. One of our grandchildren, Angela, also graduated from San Francisco State University in 2019.

The Zodiac Serial Killer

1968-1969

The Zodiac Serial Killer was a killer who operated in the late 1960s. Between December 1968 and October 1969, he targeted four men and three women. The first murders attributed to the Zodiac were the shootings of high school students Betty Lou Jensen and David Faraday in Benicia while in their car on December 20th, 1968. Then in July 1969 in Vallejo, Darlene Ferrin and Mike Mageau were shot with Mageau surviving the tragedy. Cecelia Hepard and Bryan Hartnell were stabbed at Lake Berryessa in September, 1969. Hartnell survived and was able to give a description of the man with an executioner's type hood and clip-on sunglasses. On October 11th, a passenger entered a cab driven by Paul Stine at Mason and Geary Streets in San Francisco. The cab driver took the passenger to Cherry St. where he was shot, killed and robbed. There has been much speculation as to who the Zodiac Killer could be, however to this day no definite identification has been made. This case is still being investigated by the SF Police Department and local agencies.

The Zodiac Killer sent letters to the SF Chronicle and other newspapers in 1969 with cryptograms or ciphers. The first cryptogram was sent in November 1969. Of the four cryptograms, two have been solved, as of December, 2020. There have been five murders and two injured victims attributed to the Zodiac Killer. He claimed to have killed many people. I was working out of the Traffic Bureau assigned to the Solos at this time. Most policemen in the SF Police Department remember the Zodiac Killer and the hope of apprehending him, myself included.

Chapter 6

The South Van Ness On-Ramp

In the 1970s as a Solo, a number of other officers and I, with our own funds, each purchased a "hot sheet holder" that was attached to the handlebars of our assigned motorcycles. This enabled us to view and check various vehicles to see if they were stolen or wanted for other crimes while not compromising our safety as we drove our motorcycles.

The hot sheet holder was made of a clear hollow plastic material about 6 inches in diameter and the sides attached to the receptacle were round light sheet metal rings, keeping the covering in one piece. The diameter of the housing had a one-inch thin metal strip that (when putting the binder paper around and under the metal strip on both the front and back side) would secure it to the housing, after securing it with two plastic screws about five inches apart.

This device was secured to the handlebars of the motorcycle, directly facing the operator of the motorcycle. Each day, updated information concerning wanted or stolen vehicles was given out to the officers on binder or computer paper. We then attached it to the covering. A light switch on the right side of the holder would illuminate the entire housing so at nighttime, officers would still be able to see the data on the casing.

While on patrol one afternoon, I entered the South Van Ness Ave on ramp to the freeway heading Eastbound. As soon as I merged into traffic I checked, by habit, a vehicle that passed by me. It appeared on the hot sheet (a million-to-one shot). I radioed the police dispatcher for a check of this vehicle. The response: 10-30 – meaning stolen.

As I updated the dispatcher about my direction and the 10-30 vehicle's direction, I kept a significant amount of distance from the operator of the vehicle, so he would not notice me. This would give other police units time to position themselves and intercede for the capture of the suspect.

The driver continued eastbound on the freeway and then headed southbound on the James Lick Freeway. When the driver arrived directly behind SF General Hospital, he rapidly accelerated the vehicle and exited the Army Street off ramp heading Westbound — he probably knew I was pursuing him. I continued to follow the driver. It should be noted that this off ramp splits into three different locations: Army Street, Potrero Ave, and Old Bayshore Avenue.

All of a sudden, I noticed water sprayed high into the air and as I continued my pursuit and arrived at the concrete barrier that separated the three different exit locations. In this instance, several large containers filled with water protected a driver, should he strike the barrier.

The driver struck the barrier head on, totaling the entire front end of the car. The driver was standing outside of the car some distance from the vehicle. He was placed under arrest and the car was towed. I was later informed that a fatality had occurred at this very location in the previous six months. I went to the first hearing of the suspect in court the next day; the case was continued, and I was not informed of subsequent hearings or outcome of the situation.

Flies

In the 1970s, I worked the day shift on a motorcycle in the Mission District and in a stationary position at the Northwest corner of States and Castro Streets to observe traffic violations.

I was approached by a young man who stated that his landlady had not requested his rent payment on the first of the month and this was in the second week of the month. I informed him that he shouldn't be concerned because there could be a number of reasons for this. However, he further stated that there was an odor in her backyard. I again informed him that it could be animal droppings (feces), he replied, "But look at all the flies on the window."

I looked up at two different windows and observed hundreds of flies on these windows. They were inside of the curtains that hung stretched onto curtain rods. I contacted police headquarters and requested a Mission Radio Car be dispatched for a possible "802" — a death.

Needless to say, there weren't any radio cars available. No surprise there. I went to the back of the property and broke a window with my 26" baton. After gaining entry I noticed a very clean and orderly residence. Gaining confidence, I continued walking down a hallway and noticed a door ajar and as I approached the door, I stepped on some bugs which turned out to be maggots, and then noticed an elderly woman that apparently fell out of her bed and onto the floor. I immediately went down some stairs that led out to the front entrance but not before opening the door and bypassing numerous flies.

I radioed the police dispatcher and informed her of the situation and requested the coroner and a Mission Station Radio Car to my location. I received a confirmation. I preserved the scene until the arrival of the coroner, as this is the most important part of any death scene. The coroner arrived and took over the scene and the situation. It should be noted that the coroner is in charge of this type of investigation; not the chief of police, homicide unit, crime lab, not even a mayor – until the coroner turns over the investigation to one of the other units.

Later, I spoke to one of the coroners that took charge of the scene and he stated he was being transferred to inside duty and that he was going to miss being, "out in the field."

Jack Rosenbaum: "Our Man on the Town"

In the 1970s while employed as a Solo to enforce mainly traffic violations, I encountered some unusual situations.

For example, while traveling westbound on California Street between Fillmore and Webster Streets I observed a white Rolls Royce sedan make a left turn over the double lines into the Grand Central Market parking lot in violation of section 21651 of the California Vehicle Code. I entered the parking lot and approached the driver of the vehicle as he exited his car. To my surprise it was Bing Crosby, the famous actor and singer.

He was small in stature with scintillating blue eyes. I requested to see his driver's license. Mr. Crosby stated that he didn't have it with him.

I informed him I would cite him for not having his license and if he showed it to the traffic court the citation would be dismissed. Mr. Rosenbaum would write about this encounter I had with Mr. Crosby in one of his newspaper articles in a brief and humorous way. I read in the newspaper that Bing Crosby, an avid golfer, had scored a hole in one at the famous Monterey Peninsula Golf Course down in Monterey, California. Not many golfers have done this because you must hit the golf shot some 200 yards over the Pacific Ocean. He hit this great golf shot with his driver in 1947. I learned about this incident in a newspaper article.

Another time, I was writing a citation to a motorist on the northeast corner of 5th and Howard Streets when a person on the second floor of an apartment leaned out of his window, removed his false teeth, and threw them at me, striking my helmet. Again, Mr. Rosenbaum with succinct humor wrote about the incident including my name. Finally, he wrote about me in one of his columns when I pulled over a driver for a traffic violation at 17th Street and Clayton and, radioing with a police dispatcher, learned that the person had $280.00 in outstanding traffic warrants. Two blocks in to following the motorist to the police station, I observed another motorist violating a vehicle code section. I stopped him and later learned he had $255.00

worth of traffic warrants. The two motorists were escorted to a District Police Station to pay the warrants in tandem style.

Jack Rosenbaum was a San Francisco Newspaper icon for almost 70 years, who wrote over 10,000 columns. He passed away on October 21, 2007 at the age of 100 years.

Notation: After over fifty years I still possess newspaper articles written by Jack Rosenbaum. I wanted to use these articles with direct quotes. I requested copyright permission on some of these articles. After two months I received emails stating that my requests have expired, therefore the above format.

The Dan White Riots

On November 27, 1978, Dan White, a former SF Police Officer and SF Supervisor, entered City Hall and shot and killed Mayor George Moscone and Harvey Milk. Mayor Moscone had refused to give back Dan White his former Supervisor's job. Dan White often clashed with Harvey Milk, a gay activist.

After a jury convicted White of voluntary manslaughter on the night of May 21, 1979 and given a sentence of seven years and eight months based on diminished capacity, a large crowd showed up in the Castro District and then later proceeded to the City Hall. My personal experience at the riots placed the crowds well over 10,000 or more. I was a sergeant at Park Station and assigned six patrolmen to form a squad and respond to the riots, first to Castro between Market and 18th Streets. After arriving there, we noticed the entire block of Castro Street filled with demonstrators while a man was treated by an ambulance crew for a head injury.

Next, we went to 18th and Castro Streets and watched a number of people run out of the Elephant Bar, located on the southwest corner, being chased by the Tac Squad. A group of people from that location began throwing bottles and other projectiles across the street at our position. These bottles and projectiles splattered up against the building, fortunately, not striking any of us.

At this time, we were ordered to respond to Larkin Street opposite the City Hall. On our trek to this location, we saw police cars and police motorcycles on fire, store windows smashed, looting, and vandalism along Market Street. A "406," that was called over the police radio was the most serious and life threatening call and very seldom used. There were numerous of these calls. When we arrived at our designated location we integrated with other units to form a line of about 30 officers led by Captain Cornelius Murphy — who later became the SF Chief of Police.

An order was issued to advance toward City Hall. Rioters were trying to enter City Hall by using hammer-like instruments to strike the gold leaf iron barriers that protected the entrances. As we advanced a few paces, I heard a whistling sound in the air and then a foot-long object struck me on my right arm causing my arm to collapse and remain at my side with what felt like a million ants crawling on my arm. I looked down at the pavement and observed the object that had hit me; it was a foot-long piece of concrete reinforcement rebar. Some arrests were made.

I was transported to St. Francis Hospital for examination and treatment. Notwithstanding the injury, I only required a medical sling for my right arm. At the hospital I saw many other officers with various injuries. After my treatment, I reported off duty and was placed on disability status for six weeks. I learned that many demonstrations begin peacefully even to this day but in my opinion, there are people intent on violence, some not interested in a peaceful demonstration or their cause.

Dan White would serve five years of his seven year and eight-month sentence. He died by suicide on October 21, 1985 by carbon monoxide poisoning.

One Citation

Once as a Solo in the 1970s, I pulled over a driver for a traffic citation on Old Bayshore Highway near Leland Avenue. I parked behind the vehicle, which was adjacent to a gas station, and as I approached the driver's side of the vehicle, a person who worked at the gas station approached me and told me in no uncertain terms to move my motorcycle out of the station's driveway even though the rear of my motorcycle was only a few feet in the station's driveway. I complied, issued a citation to the driver and left the area.

A few months after this incident, on Christmas Eve, I was assigned on the 7 p.m. to 3 a.m. shift to the outer area of Geary Blvd. It was a very cold evening. In fact, I placed a newspaper under my Motorcycle jacket to keep warm. There was hardly any traffic and giving a traffic citation on Christmas Eve was not something I wanted to do. However, later in the evening a car westbound on Geary Blvd near 40th Avenue was going 40 miles-an-hour in a 25-mile-an-hour zone. I pulled the operator over and requested his driver's license. To my surprise it was the same person who told me to move my motorcycle from the gas station driveway. This was a citation that I didn't feel guilty about, and it was the only one I issued that evening.

A Knock On the Door

One early afternoon while traveling Eastbound on Post Street and approaching the Miyako Hotel located at 1625 Post Street, I was flagged down by a man waving his hands above his head in my direction. I approached him and he informed me that a maid cleaning the rooms found a gun in one of the rooms underneath a pillow.

The hotel manager agreed with me that we should go to this room and check out the circumstances. Once we arrived at the door of the hotel room, the manager knocked on the door several times without any response from within. He opened the door with a master key, and we entered the room. We found a man dressed entirely in green clothes and green alligator shoes lying on his back on the bed with his arms placed behind his head. He was silent when we asked him if we could look around his room; no response. The man was handcuffed for our safety. I located and took possession of the weapon.

I then checked the closet and located a small briefcase that contained several California Driver Licenses, some money, and a white powdery substance – probably heroin - packed into several prophylactics. The man was placed under arrest. I summoned transportation from the Northern Police Station and when the officers arrived, they took the suspect into custody and the confiscated evidence as well. They also stated they would handle the booking procedure, booking of evidence, and report writing.

I later learned that all charges were dismissed because of the 4th Amendment of the US Constitution --- illegal search and seizure laws. At least the gun, narcotics, and other contraband were hopefully confiscated.

A Man in Uniform

Chapter 7

In the Line of Duty

San Francisco Police Officers Killed in the Line of Duty

Since the inception of the SF Police Department, over 100 police officers have been killed in the line of duty. In a two-year period from 1970-1971, seven police officers were killed. A plaque on the first floor of the Hall of Justice shows the names of these officers.

On June 19, 1970, Officer Richard Radetich was killed in the line of duty while writing a traffic citation in his patrol car. He was 25 years old, small in stature, a gentleman, nice looking, and was neat and well dressed. I personally knew him when he and I were assigned to the Traffic Bureau. This is a special memory in my career to reflect on. No one was held accountable for his death.

A day or two later, I was called into the Lieutenant's Office and told to drive to the Officer's residence, in another county, and bring his wife back to the Hall of Justice. They had a young daughter. This was a difficult assignment for me as I drove what seemed like a very long time back to San Francisco. It was a tragic time for his wife.

A suspect in the homicide was an ex-convict who was extradited from Ohio, but the charges were dropped due to the lack of evidence. Rest in peace, Richard.

The Zebra Killings

On October 19, 1973 in San Francisco, a couple walking down Telegraph Hill were kidnapped by a group of black men and placed in a van; the woman died but the man survived. These killings began a reign of terror that lasted six months, killed 15 people, and wounded eight to ten others. The gunmen were African American and the victims were mostly white. This appeared racially motivated toward White Americans. One victim was former SF Mayor Art Agnos. One Anthony Harris, having known these men, notified police of the suspects. Seven were arrested but some had to be released for lack of evidence. However, at trial in 1976, four men were convicted of 1st degree murder and given life sentences. At that time, it was one of the longest trials in California history. As of this writing, three men have died and one, Larry Green, remains in prison.

During that time, another police officer and I were assigned to a radio car with shotguns. There were numerous policemen in radio cars specifically for other similar situations. I remember parking on

Geary Boulevard near Divisadero Streets with another officer (Lee Clark) in anticipation of any crimes connected to these perpetrators so we would be able to apprehend them.

Park Police Station

After passing the written examination for Sergeant in the San Francisco Police Department, I was assigned to Park Police Station located at 1899 Waller Street in San Francisco. When I arrived at Park Police Station (Co. F), I was met by Sergeant Gordon Hendrickson who was a classmate of mine at Holy Name Grammar School in the 1940s. After our cordial meeting, he took me down to the basement where supplies were stored and showed me a large book that recorded incoming phone calls and other assignments that police officers were given. The blood splattered book was embedded with shrapnel, staples, and numerous bullets caused by a homemade bomb that was placed on a window ledge outside of the station, killing Sergeant Brian V. McDonnell, 44, while he sat at the station keeper's desk. Hendrickson stated he was upstairs getting dressed when the bomb went off. Coming downstairs he described a bloody scene. Outside the station an officer was blown over a police car when the bomb went off. Eight other officers were injured and one officer lost an eye. Some officers never returned to work. This took place on February 16th, 1970 just before 11:00 p.m.

There were other incidents of officers being targeted during this time frame. For example, Sergeant John V. Young was killed on August 29, 1971 while he was working at Ingleside Police Station. A shotgun was placed inside the plexiglass bulletproof window that was used to speak to persons coming to the station for police purposes. I knew and learned at that time of a civilian station aide who was cowering under a desk as she was also being targeted; she survived her injuries.

Days later I would be one of the police officers assigned to the motorcade that would escort Sergeant Young's remains to the cemetery. The motorcade stopped in front of the Sergeant's home in the outer Sunset District to pick up his wife. The Black Liberation Army and The Weather Underground were targets of responsibility. There was another bombing in front of St. Brendan's Catholic Church located at 29 Rockaway Ave, in San Francisco on October 19, 1970, at a funeral for slain San Francisco Police Officer Harold Hamilton. No injuries were documented.

It wouldn't be until 37 years later, on February 16, 2007, that the memorial would be held at Park Police Station. A plaque bears the

Sergeant's image and a short description of the event. I was privileged to have been at the ceremony honoring our fallen comrade. The crime is still unsolved.

As a sergeant at Park Police Station, there were inside duties as well as patrol car and "foot beat" assignments. On one of my foot beat assignments with another patrolman, we were walking on Haight Street when a man standing in front of his antique shop said, "Sergeant, come inside I want to introduce you to someone."

When we entered the store, this man introduced us to his wife who was a prisoner in Auschwitz when she was 13 years old. Her husband told his wife to show us her tattoo that was on her inner arm with a number in a dark blue color. His wife remained silent during our conversation. Having grown up and remembering World War II as a youngster with a grandfather from Heidelberg Germany, and a brother in the United States Navy during the war gave me profound sympathy for this person.

Another incident reminded me of a conversation with Ron Landberg, who was a spokesman for the White Panthers, named in solidarity with the Black Panthers. A book by Katherine Powell Cohen entitled *Images of America, San Francisco's Haight-Ashbury* includes a picture of me and another patrolman speaking to Ron Landberg.

Me Speaking with White Panther spokesman Ron Landberg

One afternoon a young man came to the station with a backpack that was covered with blood. As the station keeper, I spoke to him through a plexiglass window that had a small circular space for conversation. I took his name, address, and other information. He stated that he found this backpack in Golden Gate Park near Alvord Lake which is just West of Stanyan Street. I examined the backpack in front of him and recorded its contents, which would be forwarded to the property clerk's office at 850 Bryant Street. Sometime later, another man came to the station and spoke to me and stated that he noticed a man near Alvord Lake with a bloody blanket covering his entire body.

At this time, after gathering his personal information, another police officer and I responded to the area in question. We located the person under the blanket and in removing the blanket, discovered a headless torso. Viewing this horrific scene, I called for the coroner and the homicide unit. I was surprised that the diameter of the spinal cord was, to me, only less than one inch. It wasn't until two weeks later that the head was found in Golden Gate Park and was transported to the coroner's office. I never learned later of any other facts concerning the situation.

The Flower Children

During the summer of 1967, *The Summer of Love* began when mostly young people began wearing hippie fashions of clothing, listening to and playing hippie music, using hallucinogenic drugs, and taking anti-war positions — especially regarding the Vietnam War. They were also known as a free love culture and sometimes referred to as "flower children," who converged in the Haight Ashbury District (see SF Police boundaries of Haight Ashbury District). I worked at Park Police Station during this era.

Some of the popular musical groups at that time were The Grateful Dead, Janis Joplin, and Jimi Hendrix, to name a few. It is said that as many as 100,000 people converged in the area of the Haight Ashbury during this phenomenon. For example, they gathered in Sharon Meadows, (now known as Robin Williams Meadow) – a very large grassy area on the South side of Golden Gate Park west of Stanyan Street near Kezar Drive.

In 2017, Gloria, some family members, and I visited the De Young Museum, and saw displays where mannequins donned "hippie" clothing that was worn during this era, as well as written history of the time. Since I worked at Park Police Station for seven years, I had many contacts with the flower children and hippies. Much of the interactions took place along Haight Street, the most occupied area of the Haight. To see this exhibit after so many years brought back many memories and personal experiences as I interacted with the counterculture.

An Assault

I need to preface my story: At Park Station there happened to be a small building directly behind the main building. The small building contained supplies and some weightlifting equipment, including a weight bench. Assigned to inside duty with a station's aide, I answered telephone calls and wrote reports from people who came to the station. As Station Keeper, I had the opportunity to walk only a few feet to enter that other building.

After 20 years of weightlifting, I sustained a weight of 185 lbs. Later however, it decreased to 175 lbs. When station duties were quiet, I simply walked around to the back of the building and would bench press. It only took a few minutes while keeping me in good physical condition with my other exercises.

One early morning at approximately 3:30 while on patrol in a radio car and driving West on Waller Street (and approaching Stanyan Street) I looked to my right and observed a halfway house with a recessed driveway. A woman lying on her back was being assaulted by a heavy man (maybe 200 lbs.). I immediately called for assistance (Code 2) and then hurried to the assault and was able to overcome the suspect, handcuff him, and place him under arrest. A patrol wagon with two officers arrived and transported him to Park Station for booking. I learned later that the suspect was sent to prison for two years. A just sentence?

Weightlifting paid off! In all 30 years in the San Francisco Police Department I never once used excessive force. I only used the force necessary to overcome the resistance. I'm proud of that.

A Back up Situation

While assigned at Park Station and having the rank of sergeant in the 1980s, I heard a call over the police radio that sent two officers from Park Police Station on an assignment on McAllister Street regarding a man that had two outstanding warrants for his arrest. I radioed to headquarters that I would back them up. Upon my arrival and after ringing the doorbell I gained access to the residence and climbed about twelve stairs and met the other two officers who were speaking to a woman and a man.

The woman wanted the man out of her residence. I asked the man what his name was and he refused to answer. I noticed he had the outline of a wallet in his back pocket. I patted him where the wallet was and asked him to show me his identification. He stated, "get your f….n hands off me." I placed my hands on him to restrain him and see if I could ascertain his identification when he resisted. A struggle ensued and I remember him grabbing the handle of my gun. His resistance was finally overcome with the other officers assisting me.

A call for backup was initiated and two more officers responded and took the suspect to Park Station. Additional information was obtained from the woman regarding this person. Before leaving the residence one of the police officers asked, "Whose gun is this?" and bending down I picked up the gun. It was my weapon.

The holster that I had was a "break away" front holster which had a slit down the front enabling the person carrying the weapon to draw it straight forward from its holder (a quick draw). At Park Police Station, the suspect was very cooperative and was booked for the outstanding warrants and for resisting arrest.

Chapter 8

A Suspicious Occurrence

As a Solo in the 1970s and traveling Westbound on California Street between Webster and Fillmore Streets, I observed a tall thin young man running extremely fast South on Middle Alley (located midblock between Fillmore and Webster Streets). When he arrived at California Street, he turned right and continued running in a westerly direction.

When he arrived at Fillmore Street, he turned right and continued, this time running North until he reached an alley on the West side of Fillmore. I yelled at him to stop several times but to no avail. I radioed police headquarters to ascertain if there were any illegal activities going on, with negative results. As I pursued him westbound on this alley between California and Sacramento Streets, he suddenly turned around and began running in the opposite direction toward Fillmore Street. It took me extra time to turn the motorcycle I was riding because of the narrow dimensions of the alley.

Once this man arrived at Fillmore Street he turned right and began running South. At this time, I noticed a Muni Inspector, in uniform, in the area so I yelled to him to grab the person and restrain him. After the person was restrained, I handcuffed him behind his back and patted him down. When I got to his right ankle inside his sock was a large amount of cash.

At that very moment, a call from the police dispatcher broadcasted: "All cars, a hold-up alarm at Sacramento and Fillmore at Fulcrum Savings and Loan." I informed police headquarters that I had a suspect in custody and to cancel other units that were responding to the scene.

I requested transportation to take the suspect to Northern Police Station. Once at the station, the FBI arrived and the investigation was turned over to them. They told me this person had committed a robbery about six months prior. The money retrieved was marked money taken from the savings and loan. Case closed.

General Patton

While assigned to the Solo Motorcycle Unit and under the command of Lieutenant Jeremiah Taylor, I was notified that a weapon inspection was going to take place on the 5th floor of the Hall of Justice. Lieutenant Taylor was an immaculate man, bald headed, strong in stature, and with motorcycle boots and attire, he appeared to me to bear a likeness to General Patton.

On this particular day, we responded as told to the 5th floor of the Hall of Justice for the weapon inspection. It should be noted that the fifth floor was used as a gym. The floor of the gym had hardwood floors.

Lieutenant Taylor ordered us into formation and attention to inspect our weapons. This was highly unusual, as we had never before had such an inspection. The command was given to "present arms and unload weapons." This, properly done in accordance with our police manual, would necessitate us drawing our revolver weapons muzzle in a raised position pointing toward the ceiling, elbow bent, ejecting the live rounds from the weapon by using the ejector rod of the gun, and using the other hand in a cupped position to catch the live rounds.

When the order came for the inspection and unloading of the guns, all that could be heard were bullets falling onto the hardwood floor. Perhaps more practice?

Kidnapping

While on motorcycle patrol in the early morning hours and driving south on South Van Ness Avenue nearing 26th Streets, I noticed a car parked facing west in a driveway, but the rear end of the car was partially in the shoulder blocking some of the sidewalk. When I looked into the passenger side of the car, I observed a sizable amount of blood on the rubber floor mat.

With a flashlight in hand, I checked the rest of the interior of the vehicle and observed a man lying apparently asleep in the rear seat. He was awakened and deemed to be under the influence of alcohol. It should be noted that at that time in the late sixties, a SF municipal code section 67 made it a violation to be, "in or about a motor vehicle under the influence of alcohol." I arrested this man and called for transportation so he would be transported to Mission Station. The vehicle was towed.

When I arrived at Mission Station for the booking process and while his property was confiscated, I noticed that he possessed another man's wallet and other property. I looked at the teletypes to see if another crime had been committed with negative results. This other property was booked separately for future identification.

The following evening, I checked the teletypes and read that a man had been assaulted, robbed, kidnapped, and his car stolen. This man had been found unconscious and taken to Mission Emergency Hospital. The car and property that I had booked belonged to the victim. Later, the victim awoke and reported the incident. I contacted another solo motorcycle officer, Hobart Nelson, and informed him of the circumstances and asked him if he would assist me in going to the suspect's residence and arresting him; he agreed.

We went to the residence in the Mission District, placed the suspect under arrest, and had him transported to Mission Station for the booking process namely; kidnapping, robbery, and auto theft. About six months later at trial he was found guilty of all charges and was sent to state prison.

Judge Joseph Kennedy

Once in the 1970's, I was assigned a standard court day for a person protesting a citation that I had given. My court date at that time was a Friday. Since I did not work a day shift, I appeared in court either in a sport coat and tie or a suit and tie. After testifying and the case adjudicated, I was given four hours of compensation and allowed to go home, which was the procedure at that time.

A former public defender, Joseph Kennedy, was appointed to the Municipal Court Bench as a Judge in the 1970s. He was an eloquent speaker with a South African accent. One day after I testified in his court and the case was adjudicated, I was dismissed from court. As I rose from the witness stand, Judge Kennedy leaned over and in a soft voice asked me if I wanted to retire to his chambers after court was adjourned for some refreshments. I gladly accepted his invitation and waited for the court to adjourn. In the Judge's chambers there were all kinds of beverages and alcoholic spirits to enjoy. It was an unusual but enjoyable experience as we exchanged pleasantries.

Chapter 9

A Grave Situation

While I was working the Day Shift at Park Station, a woman holding a small child came to the station to report that her boyfriend had assaulted her and had a gun. She further explained that she told her boyfriend that she was going to the police station to inform the police about the assault. His reply to her: "f — the police." I brought her into the station while other police officers and I checked his record. He did have a criminal record.

Their residence was located on California Street on the North side near Masonic Avenue. It was a flat with twelve steps to the upper residence. I, as the Sergeant, along with two plainclothes officers and two uniformed officers, went to the residence to try to resolve this serious situation. I received the key to the residence from this woman and we all responded to the residence. The woman with the child would remain in the police car until the situation was resolved.

After arriving at the location, I had the two undercover officers stationed in the backyard while the two uniformed officers were stationed behind me as we arrived at the top of the stairs. I knocked on the door with no response. (I said to myself, thank goodness!).

I knocked again even though I had obtained the key from the victim. Just then a man opened the door slightly before opening it wider, at this time he held a handgun placed against his right temple; his eyes were glazed and blurry. He said, ``I'm not going back.'' I replied, "Who said you were going back?" in an attempt to calm the situation down. Also, at this very moment one of the officers behind me called, "Code 33 (emergency). Man with a gun."

I was only a few feet away from the man when he pressed the weapon up against his right temple and discharged it. Immediately he fell face forward, like a tree having been cut down. Blood like a river flowed from his head with the gun falling away from his side.

An ambulance was immediately summoned and they arrived shortly after, placing him in the ambulance to be taken to Mission Emergency Hospital. The ambulance crew told us that they would respond to the hospital with utmost care and minimum speed so as not to cause any further injury to his head. The wound was subsequently fatal.

Robert Hooper

In the 1970s I first met Officer Robert Hooper, who was a Solo like me. Before that, he served our country in the United States Marine Corps.

Officer Hooper was a humorous gentleman with a giddy laugh; he was a man of the highest integrity. We became friends.

One day while he was on patrol on 3rd Street, he pulled over a motorist for a traffic violation and after he got off the motorcycle and approached the vehicle, the driver got out of the car and shot Officer Hooper in the chest, knocking him down. Hooper got up and returned fire, but did not strike the suspect as he fled. At that time, Hooper had purchased his own bulletproof vest, which probably saved his life. The suspect got away but was later caught and sent to the State Penitentiary. Hooper personally told me that he only sustained a bruise on his chest. He was given time off for his injury. After this incident the entire department was issued bulletproof vests.

Robert Hooper and I worked together occasionally when inclement weather was prevalent and we were assigned to a radio car for accident investigation. On another occasion, we were detailed to a firing range in Pacifica to practice with AR-14 assault rifles. At the firing range when a round was discharged the dirt from the round would cause dirt to fly in the air and then the sound of the weapon would be heard; approximately at 1,125 feet per second.

On the way back to the Hall of Justice we stopped at Estrada's in Colma for lunch. Today this building is considered a landmark.

Sometime later in the evening of Thursday, February 9, 1978 while on patrol, Officer Hooper pursued a vehicle for driving recklessly and failure to stop. The suspect fled and drove to his residence in the Sunset District and went inside.

After the vehicle was located, when Officer Hooper and another officer attempted to enter the residence, the suspect opened fire, striking both officers and killing Officer Hooper. He is survived by his wife and three children. I think of him often. He served his country and the people of San Francisco. Rest in peace.

The USS Coral Sea

While working in the San Francisco Police Department in the 1970s, the United States Navy invited the San Francisco Police Department and the San Francisco Fire Department to board the Aircraft Carrier USS Coral Sea. Gloria and I and our three children accepted the invitation and boarded the ship in Alameda. It was a 16-hour excursion. Sandwiches and Kool-Aid were provided along with a large band to entertain us. The flatbed elevator took us up to the flight deck where planes were docked. We were able to view a show of helicopters and maneuvers by the aircraft.

One experience I will never forget was the announcement over the PA system that a Phantom Jet was approaching from the West at 9:00 o'clock. We were on the flight deck when this jet passed by the aircraft carrier at approximately 500 yards to the port side, and as it passed the ship there was no sound because it was breaking the sound barrier–then the sound of an explosion. It then climbed straight into the air. The afterburners were visible as it climbed out of sight.

The entire experience was unforgettable as we docked back in Alameda at about 7:30 pm that evening. It also brought back memories of my brother, Wendel, who – as a third year student at San Jose State University majoring in music – joined the United States Navy the day after Pearl Harbor was bombed. As a signal corpsman he completed his service and was released in 1945 after the war. Sometime later he gave me one of his navy uniforms.

My mother received the American Flag from the US Navy when my brother died. After my mother's passing, I took possession of the flag. My brother is buried in Oak Hill Cemetery in the Veteran's Section of the cemetery. My mother and her sister are also buried there.

Chapter 10

Weapon Confiscation

I was a Solo on my motorcycle Northbound on Potrero Avenue approaching 26th Street, and I pulled over a male suspect driving a stolen car. Once the vehicle was pulled over and in a stationary position, the driver was placed under arrest and handcuffed; I requested assistance from the radio dispatcher in transporting the suspect to the City Prison and help in towing the suspect's car.

Two officers I knew from the Traffic Bureau responded to my location. We located a gun in the vehicle. After completing the investigation and other required police procedures, I suggested to the other officers that we should flip a coin to see if one of us could petition the judge handling the case for possession of the weapon and then we could petition our chief for the weapon. We all agreed and I won the flip of the coin toss.

At court the judge granted the petition for me to take possession of the gun. Now one final step; I contacted the Deputy Chief of Police, Al Nelder, and he asked me, "You don't have a backup gun, do you? I replied, "No sir," and he signed a paper form authorizing me to take possession of a 38 caliber Police Special Smith and Wesson 4-inch barrel. Sometime later, I had this weapon "reblued," that is with a deeper blue color, enhancing its appearance and value.

Embarrassing

After I got married and when I was in my early thirties, I began running approximately three miles daily. I entered some running events such as Bay to Breakers. The distance is about six and one half miles from near the Ferry Building to the Great Highway in San Francisco. The course ran West down Howard Street to 9th Street, crossing over Market Street onto Grove Street, then West up and over

Grove Street which was challenging for me, due to the steepness of the hill.

Arriving at Divisadero Street, the course turned onto Fell Street, then through Golden Gate Park on Main Drive until reaching the Great Highway. In May of 1972 my time was 1:06:31 and on the other occasion my time was 57 minutes. I remember on one occasion when assigned to the two-wheel motorcycle unit, I was assigned to follow the lead runner so as to keep the integrity of the race. The lead runner was running each mile at about five minutes per mile. Ken Moore, a noted runner, won this race several times. In 1972, his winning time was 36:39 seconds.

I also ran the Lake Merced Run, which is about four and a half miles around Lake Merced. My times on four different occasions were not documented, but I received one medal and three ribbons: May 3, 1975, December 20, 1986, December 18, 1987, December 18, 1988, and one other.

While assigned as a Sergeant at Park Police Station in 1978, I was concerned about patrolman, Joe Perrone, who smoked continuously. He was a barrel-chested man with a commanding appearance. One day I told him he should stop smoking because it wasn't good for him. I was 45 years old and with all the running I had done in the past, I felt I could win a race with him and this would convince him to stop smoking.

Joe Perrone was about 35 years old. I told him, since I was running every day—in fact my best three mile run was 19 minutes and 15 seconds, which is approximately six and one half minutes per mile — and because of his smoking, I felt that I could probably beat him in a 440-meter race. He accepted the challenge and the race was set for a date a month in the future inside Kezar Stadium. The day arrived and several other policemen entered the stadium to witness the event. It was embarrassing to say the least, as Perrone outran me from the start to the finish, leaving me in the dust. So much for shooting my big mouth off.

It's interesting to note that exercise affects blood pressure. Dr. Karl Lee, our family doctor, informed me of several interesting facts regarding blood pressure. The following information by Dr. Lee states, "Blood pressure will go up during exercise up to but less than 200 in a normal person. Thirty minutes after exercise, the blood pressure is at its lowest point, below the baseline. Blood Pressure lowers because the blood vessels dilate during the exercise to get more blood to your muscle to bring more oxygen.

On one occasion I took my blood pressure before taking a rigorous bicycle ride for approximately 45 minutes. My blood pressure before the exercise was 120 over 88. After the exercise it fell to 110 over 70. Later the blood pressure will return to its previous reading. Common sense tells me that the vessels expand and improve the flow of blood to the arteries too. Just healthy.

Chapter 11

The Friendly Skies

After retiring from the San Francisco Police Department in 1988, I applied for a job at United Airlines and was hired in March of 1989. I was assigned to Ground Support at the San Francisco International Airport.

The part time job began at 10:00 a.m. and ended at 2:00 p.m. After being hired, my first assignment was at the Wide Body Kitchen on Mitten Road in Burlingame where we would load food carts onto trucks for outbound flights and unload food carts from the inbound flights. Drivers needed a commercial license to drive the trucks. The beds of the trucks were able to be raised to position it to the entrance to the doors of the aircraft. Before work at the Wide Body Kitchen we enjoyed fresh orange juice, cranberry muffins, and coffee. Starting pay was $9.00 dollars per hour and would eventually reach $16.00.

However, included in the salary were flight privileges, stock, medical, dental, and a 401K plan. If a person reported for work for six months without being sick, late, or injured, that person would receive a flight pass anywhere in the world without any service charges. A person could also choose to receive a US Savings Bond in the amount of $100.00 instead of the flight privileges if so desired.

Gloria and I and our youngest son, Joe, who was under 18 years old at the time were all eligible for flight privileges and medical coverage. On one occasion, Joe was able to fly First Class to Switzerland and return to San Francisco in Business Class. Gloria and I traveled worldwide using our flight privileges, and on some occasions we would be fortunate to fly First Class.

Some of our flights were not without anxiety. For example, while in France we were at the Charles De Gaulle Airport waiting to fly back to San Francisco when an airport employee told us there was no plane available, but there would be an extra flight the following day. The next day we flew Business Class back to San Francisco. Another example was when Gloria and I were in Amsterdam when United's only flight back to San Francisco was full and we needed to get a hotel for the night. I informed Gloria that if there was only one seat available for the next day's flight that she would take it and that's exactly what happened. The following day, I flew out of Amsterdam via Business Class to Washington D.C.'s Dulles Airport. When I arrived at Dulles, I had to wait two hours for my connecting flight to San Francisco. Instead of purchasing a beer I took a van across the airport and had my shoes shined. Back at the gate of my departing flight, there was a long line waiting for boarding.

After the passengers boarded the flight they called my name and I received my ticket. I looked at the ticket and the seat assignment was 1D—First Class. Before we flew out of the airport the flight attendant asked me if I wanted anything and I replied, "a Heineken, please." In fact, I had two!

Another time we missed our flight to Hawaii but my golf clubs were placed on that plane. We made the next flight only to find out when we arrived in Hawaii that my golf clubs didn't arrive there due to mechanical problems on the original flight. The airline stated that the clubs were due to arrive the following day, and they did. I played in the United Airlines Golf Tournament. There is stress in "standby" circumstances.

Golf was an enjoyable recreation, bringing camaraderie and social friendship. There was one occasion, however, where it was not so. After playing in a tournament at Sharp Park Golf Club, I placed my golf clubs in the trunk of the car, changed into my street shoes and headed home up Sharp Park Road in an Easterly direction on the windy two lane road headed toward Skyline Boulevard. There was a vehicle next to me in the right lane when I suddenly felt a sharp pain on the inner part of my right wrist. As I tried to drive carefully and at the same time discern what was causing the pain, I looked at the area and observed a bug latched onto my skin. With some difficulty, I eventually pulled it out of my skin, crushed it and placed it onto the center of the console area. At home I discovered the area of the bite was red and circular the size of a dime. In the center of the red area was also a smaller circular area in a black like color. It is often described as a "bullseye."

I later learned it was a tick and these types of bites can cause Lyme disease. Our son-in-law, whose father was a doctor, convinced me that I had extracted the entirety of the tick, so I chose not to go to the Emergency Room—perhaps not the right decision. Some of the bites can cause joint pain for extended periods of time. For example, Leslie Griffith, the KTVU anchor on the 10:00 p.m. news for many years (which Gloria and I watched regularly) died in Mexico on August 10, 2022. She had been bitten by a tick in Oregon in 2015. She was confined to her bed on many occasions because of this. Reading about her demise reveals that her death was attributed to Lyme disease.

Not all ticks carry Lyme disease. Infected blacklegged ticks transmit the disease. Mine, fortunately, was not the case. I probably got the tick while looking for a golf ball after hitting an errant shot into some shrubbery. No more looking for golf balls in these areas anymore. I once met a man walking his dog on the Sharp Park Golf Course and during our conversation he stated when he got home his dog would be covered with ticks. A good suggestion would be carrying some tweezers in a plastic sandwich bag, removing the tick, which can be difficult, and then going to the emergency room so they can evaluate the bug.

Another exciting trip Gloria and I had with our son, Joe, was to Mazatlán, Mexico. We flew out of Los Angeles on Mexicana Airlines Boeing 727. On our way to Mazatlán, we made a scheduled stop in Cabo San Lucas. Before arriving in Cabo, the door to the flight crew was open (prior to 9/11) so our son went up to the flight crew and started talking to the crew.

After some time, they told Joe they would allow him into the cockpit with them while they landed in Cabo San Lucas. After seeing that our son was welcomed into the cockpit, I also went to the cockpit and after some conversation and mentioning that I worked for UAL, they informed me that they would allow me to stay in the cockpit while landing in Mazatlán. This was quite an experience. The cockpit crew consisted of the pilot, co-pilot and navigator. Before landing in

Mazatlán the crew were speaking English, but just before the landing the crew began speaking Spanish as they called each critical maneuver. This was a very exciting experience and a privilege.

––––––––––

I played in the UAL Golf Tournament in Honolulu each year for over 15 years. Once I flew by myself, played golf the next day and after the golf tournament, flew home in First Class. One other instance stands out when Gloria and I traveled to one of the golf tournaments. When driving a Budget rental car from Waikiki to Leilehua Golf Course, I observed a wooden plank in the roadway. In trying to avoid striking the object I was unable to change traffic lanes due to the traffic next to our car and drove over the object, striking it and heard a loud noise that emerged from the bottom of the car. I looked in the rearview mirror and noticed a stream of white fluid from the rear of our car going onto the roadway. Cars drove next to our car and were honking at me, bringing the situation to my attention. I then noticed the gas gauge that had been full starting to go toward empty. Having about fifteen minutes to arrive at the golf course I decided to keep going.

When we arrived at the entrance of the golf course the car stopped, having run out of gas. Some people helped me push the car a few feet into a parking space. I called Budget, and then checked into the golf tournament while Gloria waited for another car. Budget arrived and gave us a replacement car; no charge.

I have also visited the USS Arizona Memorial and looked at the names inscribed on the marble wall - 1,177 Sailors and Marines. Oil still bubbles up from below the memorial to this day. A sad day in our history. My brother served on a destroyer in the US Navy during the Second World War which gave me additional memories and tributes to these fallen heroes. Rest in peace.

Surfing was always a must while in Hawaii at Waikiki Beach. Waves were always in the two to four-foot range and renting a surfboard by the hour was very affordable.

While in Hawaii, Gloria and I attended Catholic Mass at Our Lady of Peace Cathedral in Honolulu, which is a wooden structure over 160 years old and contains a reliquary of Father Damien the priest who administered to the lepers on the island of Kauai in the 1800's. The Catholic Church has declared him a saint. The Mass at the cathedral was inspirational and moving with organ music and Hawaiian wooden instruments that brought tears to our eyes.

James A. Michener's book *Hawaii,* describes how Father Damien had to yell out his confession to a priest in a boat offshore because the priest did not want to come onto the island due to the lepers. Father Damien built coffins for the deceased lepers. At the museum located behind St. Augustine Church in Honolulu, some of his carpenter tools including his miter were on display. Gloria and I went to the museum and learned that in the early days, lepers were confined and allowed only once a year to view family members through glass windows.

A Worthwhile Bicycle Ride

During an early morning bicycle ride in 2016, I noticed a bundle of cash lying in the street. I stopped, picked it up and returned home and showed Gloria the money I found. It was in the thousands of dollars. We both counted the treasure and then I drove to the South San Francisco Police Station with the money. Once at the police station I informed the station aide the circumstances surrounding the money I found. She recorded the information, gave me a receipt, and informed me that newspaper ads would be placed in an attempt to locate the owner (s). After one year if no one identified this property, I would be able to keep it.

Section 485 of the California Penal Code states, "One who finds lost property under circumstances which give him knowledge of or means of inquiry as to the true owner, and who appropriates such property to his own use, or to the use of another person not entitled thereto without first making reasonable and just efforts to find the owner and to restore the property to him can be guilty of theft."

A year went by and I was notified by the police department to respond to the police station to reclaim the property. At the police station two people counted out the money in front of me and gave me an official receipt, which I still have. An enjoyable bicycle ride indeed. I placed the numbered receipt that I received from the police department dated January 17, 2017 in a picture frame. Honesty is the best policy.

DUIs

While on duty at 2:45 a.m. working the 7 p.m. to 3 a.m. watch with the SFPD and preparing to respond to the Hall of Justice to report off duty, I was stopped on O'Farrell Street facing East at the red light at Van Ness Avenue. While waiting for the light to change to green I heard a car coming down O'Farrell Street and coming closer and closer to my motorcycle. I quickly looked in the rearview mirror and realized I was going to be hit from the rear. I immediately drove the motorcycle toward the South curb.

Once the car skidded to a stopped position where I was previously situated, I approached the driver and he appeared to be under the influence of alcohol. After a field sobriety check, which he failed, he was placed under arrest and transported to the Hall of Justice by a Northern Police radio car for a breathalyzer test. Once his car was towed, I responded to the Hall of Justice for the breathalyzer test. A sergeant administered the test, and the driver failed. He was taken to the City Prison and booked accordingly.

I wrote the arrest report and reported off duty at about 5:30 a.m. It takes about two and one half hours to make the arrest, administer the breath, urine, or blood test, tow the vehicle, transport the prisoner to a district station, and write a report. Luckily, on the way home traffic was light except for some garbage trucks.

Another incident I remember involving a DUI arrest occurred in the Richmond District. After making the arrest and completing the necessary procedures and paperwork at Richmond Police Station on 6th Ave near Geary Street, I exited the station and one block later noticed a car weaving in the traffic lanes. The vehicle was stopped and another driver arrested for being under the influence. Two DUIs in a very short time. In a newspaper article I read there are over 44,000 DUI hearings in California every year.

Another time, I was responding to the Hall of Justice for In Service Training when a car ran a red light. I came alongside the operator of the vehicle and told him to pull over. He turned his head very slowly toward me with glazed eyes. It took him over a block to finally come to a stop. I got off the motorcycle and opened his car door. He fell out of the car and onto the street. Several empty bottles of vodka were visible lying on the floor mat on the driver's side of the vehicle.

I called for transportation so he could be taken to the City Prison. I was informed by the police dispatcher that the wagon driver did not have another police officer assigned with him and that I would have to assist the operator of the wagon in taking him to the City Prison.

Once at the prison, it was necessary to hold him up by grabbing his

clothing and his belt during the booking process. He refused all three

tests that the DMV requires. Oh well, no In Service Training.

With Deputy Chief Jack Jordan

His brother Frank Jordan was Chief of Police in San Francisco

1992-1996

Post Retirement

Sometime after my retirement, I volunteered as a Catholic Eucharistic Minister at Seton Hospital in Daly City, bringing the Eucharist to the sick and the dying. Some patients were on the subacute floor (fourth floor) because they needed intensive care. Volunteering was a very rewarding experience. For example, a friend of mine had a child with Down Syndrome. One day while visiting patients at the hospital and entering room 1015 located on the tenth floor I observed this friend of mine sitting next to his son in bed.

We greeted each other and he told me his son was dying; his son was 48 years old. His son had a complexion so white that I had never seen before. The closest I could describe this color was when my son, Joseph, and I traveled to St. Louis Missouri to watch a baseball game. As we flew out of San Francisco International Airport the pilot informed passengers that because of electrical storms we would be flying a different route. During the flight and sitting next to a window, I observed from a distance a bolt of white lightning pass through a large cloud that was completely engulfed by this spectacular phenomenon.

I spent a few moments with him giving him my sympathy. Later he told me that at exactly 10:15 p.m. his son passed away. At that very moment, wind and lightning occur. He also told me that a priest stayed overnight at the hospital during his demise. To me, signs and wonders. Days later, I attended a Catholic Mass for his son. The priest stated that we all aspire to go to heaven, but the son was already there because of his innocence. To me, these are situations in life that I refer to as signs and wonders, not coincidences. My friend gave me permission to write about his situation.

I volunteered at the hospital for approximately ten years until COVID-19 affected the entire world. I usually began at 10 a.m. and stayed for a couple of hours. At noon, Mass was celebrated in the hospital's chapel. A Catholic priest, Father Kuoc, was assigned to the hospital, not only to celebrate Mass, but to minister to the sick and dying. I also assisted him at Mass and read the Scriptures and distributed the Eucharist and wine to the congregation.

It is interesting to note that a book, *A Tree Grows in Brooklyn*, by Betty Smith, was prohibited by the Catholic Church back in the early 1940s because of what would be called promiscuity. I recently read the book and found it to be enjoyable. The family in the book were poor and not greatly educated, but the mother told the children that all that was needed was to read Shakespeare and the Bible.

One particular story in the book described how one of the characters, Francie, went to her father's funeral mass and the storyline stated, "Francie believed with all her heart that at the altar was cavalry and that again Jesus was offered up as a sacrifice. She listened to the consecrations, one for his Body, and one for his Blood, she believed the words of the priest were a sword which mystically separated the blood from the body. And she knew, without knowing how to explain why, that Jesus was entirely present – Body, Blood, Soul, and Divinity in the wine in the golden chalice and in the bread on the golden plate."

Father Kuoc was from Vietnam and fled from there in the 60s. In fact, a gun boat pursued him and other people escaping from the country in a boat. They were able to successfully escape to the Philippines and eventually make it to the United States. In fact, one day after Mass, Father Quoc informed me and some other people that went to Mass that day that the person driving that boat attended the Mass – that was some 30 years earlier.

Also, after my retirement, I decided to begin playing the piano again. I purchased an upright Palatino piano. I also had it modified to be a player-piano that used compact discs and had earphones installed so as not to cause a disruption to my wife's activities. In addition, I took piano lessons for a couple of years. Besides playing sheet music I purchased "fake books" which were in the key of C – no sharps or flats. It became easy with the melody having a single note and the base notes using chords.

Some songs in the fake books were: "I Wonder Who's Kissing Her Now," "Crazy," "I Love A Piano," "You've Got A Friend," "On Wings Of Song," "Five Feet Two Eyes Of Blue" "Piano Man," and "Pomp And Circumstance." Finally, I play religious songs each day; "Lead me Lord", "Worthy Is the Lamb", and "Taste and See." The famous Saint Augustine said, "Those who sing pray twice." I would on occasions play for patients at a rehabilitation facility in Pacifica; that ceased with COVID-19.

I also joined the IPA – International Police Association – with the US Section, Region #9. Region #9 had a brunch, sometimes monthly, but with COVID-19 this became less frequent. The brunches we did have were mostly at Nick's Rockaway in Pacifica. News updates, raffle prizes, and a social gathering with friends made this an enjoyable day. The view of the ocean was another plus.

IPA members traveling abroad would often stay in the homes of other IPA members, while being escorted to visit the country's surroundings. In fact, Gloria and I hosted two police officers from Northern Ireland: a man and his wife. We took them to the Cliff House and other parts of San Francisco. Before returning to Ireland, they rewarded us with two pen flashlights with the inscription, "Royal Ulster Constabulary GC 1922- 2001."

Top of the Golden Gate Bridge

Just before retirement, I went over to the Golden Gate Bridge in uniform and met with the lieutenant assigned to the bridge and asked him if I could see the view from the top of the bridge. He granted my request on the condition that I sign a waiver releasing the bridge's authority from any responsibility; I signed the waiver. At a later date, Gloria and I, our daughter, Cathy, her husband Robert, and our son, Joe, arrived at the bridge and prepared to take the elevator to the top of the South Tower. Joe, who was 14 at the time, refused to take the offer. From sea level the height of the bridge is over 750 feet.

Those of us who wanted to–took the elevator, which only held three people, to the top of the bridge. Gloria, the lieutenant, and I entered the small elevator and after arriving at the top of the bridge ,the lieutenant went back down by himself to take Cathy and Robert to the top of the bridge. Gloria and I were left by ourselves at the top of the bridge to look at the beautiful and inspiring Bay and Pacific Ocean. It was very calm and we felt so safe.

Gloria and I were taken back down to the roadway of the bridge while Cathy and Robert were taken to the top of the bridge. It should be noted that the elevator had no windows. The lieutenant informed us that some noted foreign dignitary demanded to be taken back down after only getting halfway to the top of the bridge in the elevator. We have a photo album of pictures we took from our exceptional experience.

Gloria and I ready to take the elevator to the top of the South Tower

Gloria and I on top of the Golden Gate's South Tower – caught in a

kissing embrace

Gloria and I hanging on

Me looking out at the expanse of the Bay

Sixty Years

My barber, Nimrod Himm, of Daly City, had cut my hair for many

years. One day I learned he was very sick with cancer and his life

would be cut short. Paul Delucchi, owner of Paul's Flowers in Colma,

and a friend of Nimrod and mine, shared many golf outings together.

In fact, when I worked for United Airlines we all flew to Santa

Barbara, California. We played the famous Sandpiper Golf Course

which had similarities to the Pebble Beach Golf Course as much of the

course ran along the Pacific Ocean. After arriving at Santa Barbara's

Airport, we took a shuttle van to the golf course, which took only five minutes. After playing the course, we returned to the airport and flew back to San Francisco's Airport all in one day.

When Nimrod's health deteriorated and he was approaching his sixtieth birthday, he wished we could celebrate his upcoming birthday. Nimrod, Paul, and I decided to go to Joe's of Westlake to celebrate. Nimrod made it to his sixtieth birthday. We all sat in a booth and enjoyed a savory lunch and cake. All during this time we were laughing and crying at the same time. Real friends.

When Nimrod passed away, Gloria, and I went to his funeral in Colma. Many friends gathered to commemorate his life. Before Nimrod died, he videotaped his last words for his family and friends. Everyone at his memorial watched with tear-filled eyes. Rest in peace, Nimrod.

Battle of Guadalcanal Ship's Memorial

The USS San Francisco was a light cruiser that fought battles in Guadalcanal in World War II and was one of the most decorated ships in the war. It was launched in 1933 and carried a crew of about 1,000. Rear Admiral Daniel Callaghan, a San Francisco native who went to St. Ignatius High School, was the commander of their cruiser task force, which had two heavy cruisers, three light cruisers and eight destroyers. This ship saw extensive action in Guadalcanal. He was killed on the bridge of the USS San Francisco. There is a statue of him at his Alma Mater.

The Japanese struck on November 12th, 1942 with "Bettys," Mitsubishi torpedo bombers, coming within 50 feet above the water to strike the USS San Francisco. Fifteen men were killed and twenty-nine wounded. This ship made a major contribution in the war.

On May 27, 2019 at 11:30 a.m., a ceremony commemorating the men aboard the USS San Francisco who gave their lives during the battle of Guadalcanal was held at the ship's memorial site at Lands' End in San Francisco. Gloria and I attended the inspiring ceremony to remember their sacrifice. A small damaged section of the bridge of the USS San Francisco is at this site. It also made us proud that my brother also served in the US Navy on a destroyer during WWII as a signal corpsman.

Escape from Alcatraz

When I was at Mission Police Station on June 12, 1962, three prisoners escaped from Alcatraz Federal Penitentiary, (a maximum security facility surrounded by water). The prisoners were John Anglin, Clarence Anglin (his brother), and Frank Morris. A fourth prisoner failed in his attempt. It has been 59 years since their escape and there is no credible evidence that these men are still alive. The United States Marshal Service case remains open and active and they should be contacted if there is evidence to the contrary.

The swim from Alcatraz to the mainland is approximately a mile and a half. When I belonged to the South End Rowing Club, I swam to Alcatraz from the South End Rowing Club and also from Alcatraz to the mainland without a wetsuit. Many other swimmers have done the same. The water temperature is approximately 54 degrees, which limits how much time that one can spend in the water - maybe an hour without getting hypothermia.

Some questions I wondered about were: Was it high tide, or low tide when they escaped or even some slack tide — 20 to 30 minutes when there is no tide? Was the tide coming in or going out? Could the prisoners swim? The prisoners had a raft and paddles. Did they choose this particular date or was it a random date? Many more unanswered questions. A mystery or something missed?

On June 13, 1962 two police officers, one named Bob Checchi, were at the St. Francis Yacht Club, in the Marina District, enjoying a drink at their bar when two men came into the bar and sat near Bob Checchi and his friend. They started talking about the escape from

Alcatraz. Bob and his friend thought they would have some fun, so they started speaking about the prisoners. They mentioned that they saw them on the Marina. After joking around for some time, they left the bar and went home. The next day at Mission Station the FBI came to the station and interviewed Bob Checchi and his friend for over an hour in the downstairs lunch room. After this, many policemen placed numerous pictures of yachts, ships, and other vessels onto the walls of the station with captions like, "Is this the ship that Checchi saw?" Embarrassing to say the least.

Juxtaposing of Two Funerals

In January, 2021, a classmate of mine, Thomas Duffy, passed away. We graduated in June of 1952 from Sacred Heart High School. After graduating from high school we often saw each other at class reunions. He was a happy person and always ready to help someone out. He worked for the SF Water Department Local 38 as a plumber. His funeral was held at Holy Angels Church in Daly City. I attended the Funeral Mass, notwithstanding COVID-19. The church was full and people were even standing at the entrance of the church.

Another funeral I attended was for a retired San Francisco Police Officer, Raymond John Allen. Before entering the police department, he served in the US Military. Upon retiring from the San Francisco Police Department, he served in the Veterans' Police Officers' Association. He was 92 years of age. A vigil and rosary were held at Duggan's Mortuary, and a Catholic Mass held at Epiphany Church on Vienna Street before interment at Holy Cross Cemetery. I attended the Mass.

As the priest and coffin – covered with the American Flag – entered the church, two SF Police Officers in Class A Uniforms with American and California flags marched into the church with the coffin. After brief protocol, the officers left the church and Mass began. As Mass was celebrated, I looked around the church and noticed that there were only 11 people including myself. When Mass was over and the church emptied, I attempted to speak to a woman who was a family member of Raymond Allen. She did not wish to speak to me and was visibly upset concerning the few people attending the Mass.

When I was at the next Veterans POA meeting I requested to mention this at the meeting. The Board allowed me to address the meeting. I stated I was only giving information and facts regarding the Funeral Mass, nothing more. Gloria sent in a Mass card to the family of Raymond Allen. A few weeks later, we received an acknowledgement of our sympathy card from the family that said,

"Thank you for attending my dad's services, it meant a lot to me…"

The Hudelson Family

The above picture was taken in front of the Pacific Cafe, located on the northwest corner of 34th Avenue and Geary Boulevard. Pictured is Frank Gundry, a waiter there for over forty-eight years, Gloria, and myself. This restaurant has wonderful seafood, but also a family atmosphere. For example, if waiting for a table, complementary wine is served and on many occasions striking up a conversation with another waiting customer can be an enjoyable experience.

Copyrights and Sources

Information taken from "Program of the Day" on pages 25 and 26, dated Sunday October 24, 1954.

Article written by Lisa Martinovic in the SF Chronicle dated February 11, 2000 titled, "Charlie's Last Ride" on page 27. (Paid for copyright permission)

Chapter 3

Photo on page 53 shows Sergeant Homer Hudelson speaking to White Panther on Haight Street. Photo and taken from, "Image of America—San Francisco's Haight –Ashbury on page 100, by Katherine Powell Cohen.